STONE WORK

STONE WORK

REFLECTIONS ON SERIOUS
PLAY AND OTHER ASPECTS
OF COUNTRY LIFE

JOHN JEROME

VIKING

VIKING
Published by the Penguin Group
Viking Penguin, a division of Penguin Books USA Inc.,
40 West 23rd Street, New York, New York 10010, U.S.A.
Penguin Books Ltd, 27 Wrights Lane, London W8 5TZ, England
Penguin Books Australia Ltd, Ringwood, Victoria, Australia
Penguin Books Canada Ltd, 2801 John Street, Markham, Ontario, Canada L3R 1B4
Penguin Books (N.Z.) Ltd, 182–190 Wairau Road, Auckland 10, New Zealand

Penguin Books Ltd, Registered Offices: Harmondsworth, Middlesex, England

First published in 1989 by Viking Penguin, a division of Penguin Books USA Inc.
Published simultaneously in Canada

10 9 8 7 6 5 4 3 2 1

A portion of this book first appeared in *Special Report* magazine.

LIBRARY OF CONGRESS CATALOGING IN PUBLICATION DATA
Jerome, John.
Stone work.
1. Stone walls—Design and construction.   I. Title.
TH2249.J47   1989   693'.1   88-40420
ISBN 0-670-80195-X

Printed in the United States of America
Set in Bodoni Book

FOR THE ONES WHO ARE IN IT:

Chris, Molly, Pawnee, Tad, Ott, Becky, Hans, Linda, Willy, Ralph, Sarah's dad, Sarah, Marty (Martin S.), Gwen, Jud, Evelyn, Kate, Julie, Richard, Liz, Ed, Mott, David, Dan, Marty (Martha J.), Lynne, and the goat.

CONTENTS

PART I

SPRING

PART II

SUMMER

PART III

FALL

PART IV

WINTER

S P R I N G

P A R T   I

[I]

EQUINOX:

SNOWFALL

The vernal equinox arrives with bright and freakishly warm weather, yanking me out of the house. There's even a patch of open water on the pond, unheard of for March. I wander around, intending only to find a spot to sit and take in the sun for a while, but find myself automatically mulling over yard chores, not wanting to waste the day. With the snow finally gone, the stone wall I'd begun the previous fall is fully exposed. I decide to stack a few more stones on it—reminding myself as I do to try to pay attention to the light. Chris and I moved here, bought this place, in order to live a more sensory life. Why can't I hang on to that intent?

The stones are the same gray as the nearby woods, and I keep craning upward, as I work, comparing monochromes. A week ago I drove a hundred miles north into New Hampshire. Snow cover was still general up there, everything still all gray and black, but on the way back I began noticing traces of brown, the hint of warmth in roadside vegetation. I could see it grow richer, mile by mile, toward the red end of the spectrum—not in any solidly verifiable way, not to direct vision, but only in the haze of twigs and saplings. That subliminal tint is what I'm looking for now, a signal that relief is at hand, even though real green is six weeks away. I find myself wondering about the color spectrum for creatures that live their lives outdoors, whose visual mechanisms are tuned to different frequencies than ours. Bees' light, I understand, is not quite like birds' light. What would it be like, that broader visual access? Is this a capacity that can be trained, like a muscle?

The work and the heat of the sun soon have me unbuttoning clothing; the heft of the stones surprises me all over again, reminding me to get my own weight set before I can successfully move theirs. After half an hour I realize my winter-softened hands—and lower back—won't accommodate much more just now. I seem to remember a nice rhythm to this job, but I'm not going to get it back in this brief stint.

The dogs are pestering me to quit anyway: If I'm going to be outdoors, I'm supposed to pay attention to them, wasn't that the deal? The two of them have been circling my pile of stones at a ten-yard radius, suggesting that I knock off this boring business and come play. I agree, and begin the complicated and tender process of standing up straight again. It's time for their customary Frisbee session—a conveniently rehabilitory calisthenic for me as well, stretching out the knots of fatigue. I fetch the plastic disks and begin spinning them out in the fluky air, trying to make them hover, tantalizingly, at the limits of the dogs' range. The object of the game is to make the dogs use all their sprinting speed, then finish with a dramatic leap and catch, the doggish equivalent of a slam dunk. They demand a good quarter-hour of hard work, minimum; it does me daily good, too, just to watch. I relish, and envy, their eager athletics in the afternoon light.

Then that light is abruptly splintered as, out of nowhere, a miniature snow squall begins sprinkling dollar-sized flakes over our hillside pocket of unseasonable warmth. The low sun shines sharply underneath the squall cloud, backlighting the giant flakes so I can barely see through them; the dogs, overheated in winter coats, seize this moment to streak for the pond, and wade cheerfully in to cool their bellies. A week ago the water was solid ice. New England springtime: I sit on the wall, sweating lightly, squinting through the piebald air; the dogs loll in the pond, snapping at the descending flakes, silver spray flying as they splash. Snow continues to fall.

The stone wall is a project that has kept me squirming all winter. We live in western Massachusetts, on what was once a working farm but now is only fields and woodlot, a nice piece of land with a house on it. The old farmhouse fell into disrepair twenty years ago, so the previous owner bulldozed it and built a sound if unexceptional new one on the site. There are fine old maples and fruit trees around the house, but it sits on a sidehill knoll, the land rolling off into open fields on three sides. It's a little stark; there isn't enough demarcation. What the place really needs is a stone wall here and there to organize the open space.

The fields are empty, but the nearby woods, parceled and reparceled among succeeding waves of landowners, are threaded through with traditional New England stone fences, abandoned now and falling down, all uselessly in the wrong place, the closest of them four hundred yards from the house. We speculated about the frightful cost of having a wall moved.

It would be an exhausting business, almost a parody of human effort: tear down the old wall, haul it to the new site, stack it back up again stone by stone. Stone is another word for total: stone broke, stone cold, stone-deaf. Moving a wall would be stone *work*—hyper-work, Ur-work, mindless, brutalizing toil. Who would hire out for a task like that?

The world doesn't lack for nasty jobs—scrubbing floors, chipping paint, mucking stables. As a kid I lived in the Southwest, and particularly detested working on windmills and stringing barbed-wire fence. Moving a stone wall, though, struck me as a symbolically awful job, awful in some perfect way. And that spoke, immediately, to the contrarian in me: I had to try it. I owned a small tractor; I'd get a wagon to pull behind it, haul the rocks out of the woods myself. I'd find some old-timer to teach me the basics of building stone walls, then proceed on my own. I'd get inside this elemental task, examine it, master it. I'd take my time at it, take years if necessary—a novel approach for constitutionally frenetic me. Such a gradual approach, I proposed, would move it out of the realm of drudgery. It would get me outdoors, give me some fine exercise, make a regular break in my sedentary day. Perfect, I said confidently, still sitting on my duff.

The fantasy recalled a wonderful summer day, years ago, on a branch of the Ammonoosuc River in New Hampshire. I was skinny-dipping, following local custom. A similarly naked stranger began building a modest stone dam downstream, attempting to deepen the three-foot-deep "swimming" hole we were sharing. I joined him in the work. We kept at it for a couple of hours, hardly talking, eyes averted, two nude males standing in icy water to our shins, working away maniacally until our backs gave out. A strange wild ritual: I kept imagining

Cro-Magnon types, damming the stream to trap fish. We disassembled it all before we left. It was very satisfying.

A decade later I was seized again by the idea of similar, almost purposeless, wall-building. It was just about the dumbest piece of work I could conceive, and I took it on grinning, amused at my own perversity, full of fantasies about stone walls leading off in all directions, stringing these hills and fields together, organizing the world.

New England springtime: I sit on the wall, sweating lightly in the snowfall; the dogs loll in the pond. I credit myself with a productive hour: added n stones, not quite randomly, not extending the wall but filling in the outline of that portion already sketched out by last fall's work. Later in the spring, when I am fetching new stones out of the woods, each wagonload will push the length of the wall ahead by a couple of feet, a satisfactory inchworm progress across the field. Today, working from a pile of last season's discards, I am only touching up low spots, filling gaps, smoothing out lines. The Irish, who build stone walls even more compulsively than New Englanders, say a particularly tight, smooth wall "has a skin on it."

To get it that way is simple: you just decide the size of the wall you want and draw imaginary planes through space to mark its two sides and its top. Then you fill in the imaginary space with real stones. Envision the hole in the air that the wall makes, then fill it. A perfect wall would look as if it had been poured from concrete—and would be perfectly unsatisfying. Gives you nothing but *dimension*, says the Irishman. I'm speaking of dry wall, of course; mortar takes the interest right out of it.

Simple, but not easy. You put the stones where they go:

where they fit (sit solidly, securely link the stones on which they rest, provide a proper bed for the stones to come), and where they are needed (to fill out the dimensions of the wall you have imagined). You just have to learn to see where they go, how they fit. There is only one rule, one instruction, in wall-building: put two stones on one, one stone on two.

———

I sit on the wall, the dogs loll in the pond. My body temperature has stabilized, they are still furiously pumping surplus heat; I tried to putter slowly and steadily, they went exuberantly all-out. We quit when discomfort overcame pleasure, rubbing our respective noses in the physiology of work.

The dogs are retrievers (Molly is a golden, Pawnee a Lab outcross), and chasing Frisbees is their job. They have other duties—harassing ground squirrels, sniffing out the previous night's territorial violations, barking at the valley—but at some canine level of understanding, chasing the Frisbee is how they earn their daily bread. They are anxious, each day, until they've performed their work, and then—tired, warm, loose— they visibly relax, wandering off to stretch and roll. I imagine them kicking their shoes off, popping a beer.

The dogs give me a daily lesson in biomechanics—the physics, so to speak, of physiology. A dinner visitor, watching a great blue heron lift its six feet of wingspan laboriously up from the pond, whispers, "Good Lord, that's aviation, isn't it?" I don't know why the sight of muscle hard at work in a living thing transfixes us so, but it inevitably does. The fascination with horses hasn't overtaken me yet, but I may not be able to resist forever. Horses are nakeder than dogs; all that muscle is closer to the play of light, so you can see it work.

———

Luminous snowflakes float about me, in air that's all the wrong temperature. Puffs of warmth give way to puffs of coolness, straight off the patches of snow in the woods; the unstable atmosphere drifts from February to June and back again. In summer, floating on the pond, you can feel the breezes die and pick up again with every passing cloud, as sun and shade boil the atmospheric gases. The same engine that swirls the snow swirls the temperature. In spring the temperature charts go all spiky, the needle slashing wide arcs at wrong times of day. Spring's great amplitude. There's physics going on around here.

[2]

MARCH:

BEGINNINGS

Damn March. Spring won't settle in, winter won't unclamp: six inches of new snow, and then yesterday, daylong rain and mist, right at the freezing point. Almost warm on the face when you step out into it, but you'd better be hanging onto something, as it was busily putting down a solid coat of ice. At dawn this morning I sat over coffee and watched the sun spray stripes of fire across the hill behind the house, lighting up the tips of ice-coated tree limbs, a quarter-inch coat of crystal on every twig. I vowed to go up there and see that later: put in a couple of good hours at my desk, then head for the loop, the mile and a half of old logging roads around which I try to walk (or ski, or snowshoe) every day. All morning long the sun kept heating up, meltwater pouring off the trees so fast it sounded like rain outside my office window. I'd want a slicker—in cloudless sunshine—for my walk. Then just as my capacity to pay attention to work began to fade, so did the sun, and ten minutes before I could get out the door, a gloomy overcast rolled in.

I went anyway, out and up into the melted wet gray lacework of woods. A good day not to be skiing, there being a crust on the snow that tried to cut me off at the ankles when my boots broke through, that scattered ahead of me on downhill slopes, tinkling like handfuls of broken glass. There was a brooding, sodden breeze that—unexpectedly—did not chill: after a quarter of a mile, I was pouring sweat in the forty-five-degree air. But my head was cleared; I'd be fresh for work again after lunch.

The reason the dawn sun lays stripes across the hillside is because the hill faces north. This seems wrong. The first time I saw this place was on a rainy day, and I misplaced a turn or two on the way in; as a result, my sense of direction was wrenched ninety degrees out of phase, and I've been struggling to get the place set right in my head ever since. After eight years, north still feels like east to me.

I keep expecting the points of the compass to fall back into place someday, perhaps with a thunderclap and a great psychic lurch, but it never happens. I've got the surrounding territory aligned okay; once I reach the main road I'm back in sync. At my house, though, the sun still rises and sets in the wrong place. I stand out in the yard and think hard, trying to shift the facts to fit the terrestrial globe I carry inside my head, but I can't pull it off. Actually, there *is* a small lurch, every time I come driving up the hill. I've become fond of it; it's as if the whole place spins on its tumblers, a combination lock securing the borders against a deluded world that still thinks north is over that way.

Twenty years ago Chris and I lived in the city, working for magazines, swept up in that jokey, aggressive, distracted life: wrestling with words and paper in tall buildings under fluorescent lights. In *Old Glory*, Jonathan Raban wrote about his own flight from such a world. "In my old, city life," he said, "there hadn't been a day when I didn't sweat at the sheer fiddle of the thing: the telephone ringing, or failing to ring; the bills in manila envelopes; the rows, the makings-up; the jumpy claustrophobia of just surviving as one small valve in the elaborate and hazardous circuit of ordinary society."

That same claustrophobia drove us, one early October, to rent a car and take a weekend break from the city. Because our magazines worked three months ahead, we had already closed our Christmas issues and were thinking about the New Year, but out in the countryside, the foliage was just starting to change. We were shocked to discover, from actual physical evidence, that autumn was only now coming on, and lovely as ever, and we were shocked again at our surprise. Our work and our city life were keeping us wrenched ninety degrees out of the season. The next year we left the city for good, for what seemed like much more complex reasons, and have been trying to work our way back into a more accurate alignment with the physical world ever since. That's what I mean by a more sensory life. Part of what I mean.

We moved to northern New Hampshire, which definitely qualified as noncity, and adjusted quickly enough. Our house was in a valley running north and south, and we came to know, without ever thinking much about it, just where the sun would rise and set, over the various seasons of the year, as it marched along the ridgelines to the east and west. Such small but solid pieces of real information became surprisingly precious to us, in ways that remained generally incomprehensible, I think, to visiting city friends.

Not that there was ever any reason not to know the same thing about the sun in relation to the canyons of Manhattan. Down in the Wall Street area, around the time of the summer solstice, the sun sets directly at the end of, and perfectly aligned with, the east-west crosstown streets. Those sundowns are a glorious sight, treasured by enthusiasts of city light (and there are such enthusiasts), who make a definite effort to go view them. I didn't know, didn't bother. Some poisonous thing about the busyness of that life, or my inept handling of it, kept me from noticing things like that.

Spring won't settle in, winter won't unclamp. I can't get into the woods to haul new stones until the snow goes; I can't extend the wall anyway until I dig new footings, and the ground is still frozen. I cruise nearby roads restlessly, inspecting walls. When my neighbors use stone for landscaping—for decorative purposes—they prefer a distinctive flat local rock called Goshen stone, which is preternaturally stackable but too tidy for my tastes. I'm looking for field walls, the raw stone piled the best way it will fit and stand. There are plenty of those, too, some clearly finer than others, but I can't yet quite see why. The stones fit better, that's all, the only criterion I can puzzle out. Of course I do most of the inspecting at twenty miles per hour, one eye on the road. I also walk, though, in the woods, taking a slower look at older, abandoned walls. The problem is figuring out what I am looking at, or looking for. It is a problem I have had in other areas.

Last fall, waiting for my mail-order wagon to arrive, I tried to learn about wall-building from books, all of which insisted that footings were critical. The first course of stones, they said, must start below the frostline, or the wall won't even stand for twenty years. I was not opposed to a certain permanence, but in this climate a safe frostline is four feet down, which would require building more wall below ground than I planned to erect above it. I decided to compromise at eighteen inches—

not out of laziness, I told myself, but for lack of interest in monument-building. Which somehow left me feeling exactly the way I used to when I copied someone else's homework.

The first wall was going to fill a forty-foot gap between a row of poplars and a rose trellis on the west side of the house, a place where lawn turned indistinctly into field. It would be two feet high, rising from a three-foot base, preserving the classic three-by-two proportions of antiquity. I drove stakes at the corners and hung string to keep the lines straight, and then began, with my usual urgency, to dig—muttering, as I did, my usual imprecations. (There's no need to go at this as if you're killing snakes, you know; it isn't going to get finished in an afternoon; you might as well come to under*stand* the process. And so on.)

What finally succeeded in slowing me down was a vision of archaeological standards: vertical sides and a level bottom. My footings would be neat, and we'd see about the walls when their time came. Taking more care tricked me nicely into taking more time, which tricked me out of beating myself to a bloody pulp in the first working session.

The extra care was an elaborate waste, based on a fundamental misconception of what building walls was going to be, well, *like*. As I would discover when I actually started putting in stones: you dig the hole to fit the rock, naturally. But I didn't think of that, and it didn't matter. Shoveling sod started working my hands into shape, awakened some muscles, sprinkled a little sobriety over my fantasies. It was all going to work out, this wall-building, so long as I slowed down and took my time. Or so I told myself, before I moved the first stone.

———

Deep footings insure against the same frost that causes farmers' fields to "grow" stones. It was Tad Glover, a North Country contractor with plenty of experience with wandering house foundations, who explained this fabulous process to me. As an underground stone expands with temperature changes, he said, it shoves back soil; when it contracts again, it clears itself a thin cocoon of air space. With every thaw, moisture trickles down the sides to collect underneath. Each new freeze turns the collected puddle into a hydraulic lift, driving the stone upward. Erosion fills in below, securing the gain. The farmer has to pick the newly emerged stones out of his fields every few years, adding the winter "crop" to his existing walls.*

Freeze-thaw cycles are what peel sheets of granite off the sides of mountains, Taddy says, to carve out the spectacularly smooth exfoliated cliffs so loved by rock climbers. It's the same process that digs potholes and fractures bridge surfaces, making them bumpy before the rest of the pavement goes bad. Gravity *will* seep ice wedges into every available physical crevice; that is the rule, and if you build stone walls, or anything else that sticks out into nature, you play by it. Or you build temporarily.

I have not built a great deal, out in nature or otherwise, but what I have built has definitely tended toward the temporary. This comes from insufficient respect for the rules, a character flaw. If you tell me I have to dig down four feet for a sound foundation, I automatically think I can outsmart that, bluff my way past it somehow. (Copy someone else's homework.) If you tell me that water collects, freezes, becomes a wedge, this gives me such a coherent and sweetly reasonable picture of physical consequences that I will at least attempt to comply.

*Recent research hints that frost may *pull* stones upward—the soil freezing tight to their upper surfaces, then heaving upward—rather than pushing them. Same effect.

It gives me something concrete that I can use as an antidote to my habitual haste.

It is not powerful enough, however, to convince me to dig a four-foot ditch forty feet long and then fill it back up with carefully fitted stones just to keep a rock from falling off my wall now and then. My wall-to-be. I am fonder of old, abandoned, partially tumbled-down walls than of neat ones anyway. Maybe, I thought, I should build a wall-that-was? Pre-abandoned? This stone work business was turning out to be more complicated than I planned.

The books about building walls illustrate just what one has to do to move large stones, erect various styles of wall, handle rudimentary design and landscape problems. These books tend to be brief, there being only so many ways to tell someone to put two stones on one, one stone on two. They are thorough, but, as I discovered when I finally began putting actual stones in the ground, a little misleading. It is unavoidable: if you are sketching wall construction, you will sketch rectangular stones, cubic stones, shapes of stone that fit the principles you're trying to illustrate. You sketch rectangular excavations for footings, with vertical sides and level bottoms. That's what I dug.

When you put a stone in the ground, however, you want a hole that fits that stone, and that stone, I guarantee you, will not have vertical sides and a level bottom. The task, therefore, is to describe, with your shovel, in the earth, the shape of the stone—not just in outline but complete with its bottom contours, three-dimensional. This gets interesting. You have to examine the stone (upside down and backward, because that's the easiest way to flip it over into its hole) and then sculpt that shape into the earth. Then you roll the stone into what you hope is its accurate female mold. How well it fits is how you keep score.

The larger the stone, the more stable the foundation: good footing stones weigh a couple of hundred pounds, which is a powerful antidote to perfectionism. You are disinclined to keep hauling them back out for final touches to the shape of the hole. You don't want to take a lot of fittings. So you spend a lot of time staring at the stone, memorizing its contours, rotating it in space in your head. After a while you learn a kind of zoned-out Zen staring, your consciousness only a memory bank for storing a shape while you dig. (After I'd been doing it for a while, I found myself remembering the shapes of particular stones as I fell asleep at night.) If I had ever stared at existing walls as hard as I stared at the upside-down bottoms of footing stones, there's no telling what I might have learned. But standing there and studying an existing wall isn't going to reduce the number of times you have to lift the stones, so there isn't the same incentive.

There's a great luxury at the footing stage: the hole in the ground is workable. Later, when you're stacking stone on stone and nothing is malleable any longer, the luxury is gone. But that plasticity is what seduced me into digging fussy footings, which was truly silly. The beginning point is the stone, not the hole; the soft accommodates the hard. That's an even firmer rule than the one about frost-wedging.

———

With no wagon yet for hauling stones from the old walls in the woods, I looked for a closer source. There were stone patches here and there in the yard, some the size of washtubs; they weren't outcroppings but foundation stones from the old barn, sticking up through the topsoil that had been bulldozed over

them. My mower would just pass over them; they were hazardous to ankles. I figured they'd make good wall footings, if
there were only some way to get them out. And they were
already a lot closer to where I needed them than stones from
the woods. I chose a medium-sized one, about twenty inches
across, and began to scratch out the rest of its dimensions.
When fully exposed it proved to be a three-foot molar, positioned on end in its own slightly larger pit. I could wriggle it
perhaps an eighth of an inch. Now what?

My strongest impulse was to cover it back up and forget the
whole thing, but I fetched an assortment of pry bars and two-
by-fours, and began waggling it out. Push it one way, stuff
something down alongside it, tilt it back the other way, always
trying to gain a little upward movement: two-by-fours in place
of the freeze-thaw ice-ram, levering the thing a quarter of an
inch at a time. Way to go, Archimedes. It took about an hour
to raise it the first six inches.

But—thrillingly—the stone accelerated as it rose: the
higher it got, the better the leverage, and therefore the more
easily it moved. At its lowest point the weight had to be lifted
straight up; as it emerged (and the hole got wider) I could lift
less and lever more, until I needed only to rock it back and
forth, inserting chocks and wedges to consolidate each gain.
Raising it was a process of tiny grabs, searching always for
more grip, a kind of rock-climbing upside down, except you
use tools rather than your fingertips in the limited little pur-
chases the rock affords. And when you screw up, you don't
fall off the rock, you drop it. On yourself, if you're not careful.

Eventually the rock rested on planks directly over the hole,
a three-foot monster sitting there like a megaduck. I had trouble
believing it: there's no way I could move a weight like that,
but there it was. I rocked it up onto wooden rollers—and

quickly discovered there was more downhill slope to the lawn than I'd realized, as it immediately tried to get away, sending me scrambling for a pry bar to stab in its path. After that, getting it to the new hole was no trick at all. At one point the stone was trundling majestically along on its own, while I simply grabbed up discarded rollers from behind and slipped them in front. And, feeling a bit like an elephant trainer, tried to steer.

The revelation in the whole process was that it had never taken much force, much strength. I had expected to do a great deal of grunting and straining against more or less intractable weight, but that turned out to be pointless. If you have to strain to move the stone, you can't do anything with what you gain. You can't hold it in place long enough to secure your advantage. You may be able to manhandle a big stone with brute strength, but you want to consider very carefully what you start manhandling, because you may end up being rockhandled by it. You want to be sure you can get the stone to where you want it to go—in one move—or you are faced with dismounting from a tiger. At that point, staying put, as a concept, takes on several new levels of meaning.

With the stone suspended above its hole, clear of the ground for the first time, I felt a strange little urge to do a victory dance around it. Celebration seemed only fair. I hadn't thought I would be able to raise it. It had been a worthy and sometimes frightening opponent, with what seemed like a will of its own, which I had overcome. But what would I be celebrating? Its defeat? It was just a stone.

The stone's will is only gravity (mine is more likely a hormone). A victory dance seemed inappropriate from a conventionally repressed, otherwise non-dancing, middle-aged male for whom willfulness, like some other forceful qualities, has usually turned out to be a lousy idea (a lesson I have embraced with some relief). Stone work does keep reminding me, mystifyingly, that I am male; feeling male is also not a state I am comfortable owning up to. Very little else that I do calls gender to my attention. Yet in some way I can't identify, stone work is as masculine a thing as I've ever done, as elemental an effort as I can find to make. And, surprisingly, something about that is what makes it so satisfying. In a daily routine otherwise sedentary to the point of near-paralysis, this particular form of effort fills an unacknowledged need. Maybe it's a way of letting the genie safely out of the bottle—the one that likes to push against the world. A *little* bit out of the bottle. That genie does seem to want the world to push back. Wants resistance, wants some form of response. And stones do resist, all right.

Once, daydreaming as I dug footings, watching the shovel tip slice through clay, it suddenly wasn't me on the handle end but my late stepfather, Ott Luer. What I saw was some reminder of the skill and efficiency with which, in my memory, he handled shovels. We did a lot of shoveling together, Ott and I—drainage ditches, fencepost holes, gardens. He was good at it and I, at age twelve or fourteen, was not. This gulf was the source of endless frustration between us, my skills insufficient for the tasks he set, his skills setting an impossible standard. But then all was gulf between us anyway. Now, a ghost: Ott's hand on the shovel, rather than my own. And relief: what had once seemed a powerful skill was probably not much more than size and strength. So that's what his secret was. To become effective with things like shovels, I hadn't needed to acquire miraculous talents after all, I only had to grow up.

On second thought, no, it wasn't just size and strength, I also had to acquire a sensible grasp of the way weight and force work, of the physics of things. Ott had that, and I suspect it is the connection in my head with maleness. At least when I try to operate the physics of the world, and succeed, the moment of success feels male. Ott was a powerful and effective one of those, who entered my life after I'd luxuriated perhaps too long in female society. (I was surrounded by soft, safe aunts.) I was frightened silly of him. His power had to do with building things, making things happen. He owned power tools, maintained a workshop, took on what seemed then to be large and technical projects. He also screwed up occasionally, and I took such delicious joy in that. We didn't get along very well. I am still trying to win his approval, obviously. What we have here is stone work as psychiatrist's couch.

———

The mail-order wagon finally arrived: an axle, two wheels, a carton of girders and planks. Assembled, it was suspiciously flimsy, so I doubled the one-inch planking of the bed and walls. Easily said but uncertainly accomplished: I lack confidence that my carpentry will ever work out, go at it slapdash in order not to waste time on failures, cut corners out of cheapness—and watch the prophecy fulfill itself. The double-planking worked, or has so far, but I'll have to replace it eventually with heavier stock. In the old days they preferred a stoneboat, a crude plank sledge at ground level so you didn't have to lift the stones as far. That would have been cheaper, but I didn't think of it. Besides, I wouldn't want to cut up the ground with all that skidding.

With a functional wagon, I was in business. I hitched up and set out for the abandoned stone wall closest to the house, a couple of hundred yards up an old logging road. Began loading stones. They were, gee, *heavier*, somehow, than I expected.* I removed the top course of stones from a few feet of the existing wall, piled them in the wagon, hauled them in, dumped them beside the new footings. I tried to stack them up into new wall, but they didn't seem to want to stack. I decided that was because I didn't have enough shapes to choose from, and went back for another load.

So, I thought, here we go, building wall. Only twelve or fifteen revelations in that first load of stone: aspects of this project I had grossly underestimated or improperly conceived, matters I had insufficiently considered. About one discovery per stone, each of which represented a succession of problems—to be solved, mostly, by application of force, although the problems of selection and placement also required something else, some other kind of force—of intelligence, or judgment—that I didn't yet quite have available. Each stone was an extremely unwieldy mass of totally irregular shape, without an ounce of cooperation in it, and here I was proposing to use the damned things for building-blocks. Perhaps I should have thought this through.

That was the first load; by the second I had stopped trying to build walls at flank speed and by brute force; by the third I was beginning to see that if I planned things out a little, the process was less frequently depressing—or less frightening, anyway. I dimly glimpsed that there were skills to acquire, and tried to avoid hurting myself until I acquired them. Use the head to save the back. As for the new wall, I kept trying

---

*A small startlement to be repeated at the start of each day. Or at least there hasn't yet been an occasion when the stones were lighter than I thought they were going to be. A cubic foot of granite weighs a hundred and fifty pounds or more. A yard of wall three feet high takes roughly a ton of stone. I love that kind of talk.

stones until one of them fit, and then tried some more until another one did, and before long I'd managed to establish a reasonably square and solid beginning of a wall, leading off more or less in the direction I wanted it to go. I didn't have any idea how I'd done it, exactly—I hadn't arrived at even a first premise about how the stones were in fact fitting together—but there they were, fairly close to where I wanted them, making up something that looked about like it was supposed to look. Okay, it's possible, walls can be built. I can do this. And it didn't look too bad. Or it looked like it wouldn't look too bad when I got a little more of it done. That's the thing about a stone wall: start one and it'll drive you crazy, wanting to be completed.

My usual working day is spent in front of one of today's glorified typewriters, staring at a cathode ray tube. In my real work it is not stones but blips of light that are moved around, in search of arrangements that represent some kind of sense. As the hours pass, the room shrinks to a cocoon no larger than from screen to skull, airless. (As Johnny Bench said of the Astrodome, the molecules don't move around enough in here.) My eyes go grainy and hot, my body numb except for the small aches of inactivity that traverse my back and shoulders the way the sun's shadow creeps along a wall. Eventually I stagger up, stretch, scrub my face with my hands. If I am not too dulled to think of it, I step outdoors, where there are all new molecules, the stricter reality of a fresh temperature, other levels of moisture, wind, new sounds. The longer I've sat, the more sharply I am buffeted—invigoratingly—by the change: re-fresh-ment, simply from firing off a different category of synapses. Sets me in stone, that process in there; requires the occasional freeze-thaw cycle.

How spellbound we were by the first computers, how enthralled, sitting in dark rooms, pouring dizzying hours into those bright new screens. *Spell*, as in witchcraft; *bound*, as in receptor sites: the hacker's drug, those little pieces of light precisely fitting some unrecognized keyhole in the attention span, tripping us out of the physiology, free to go off and play without the burdensome energy demands of flesh and blood, with all its aches and pains, its pumps and tubes.

Stepping back out into the molecules reminds me how badly I am addicted. Stepping back into the physiology. Where shall I turn my efforts now? To the pleasurably exhausting (stone work), or the numbingly addictive (back to the writing machine)? What shall I be next, a tube or a blip?

[3]

A P R I L :

B I R D

T I M E

The snow went, came back, went away again, followed by a string of absolutely Scandinavian days, everything stalled in a maddeningly silver gray, thirty-four degrees around the clock. The end of March is when the bluebirds usually come back; they kept not showing up. (Forget about robins, around here bluebirds are the rock-solid concrete signal that winter's back is broken.) Mallards and Canada geese were also due, and the pond awaited them, ice-free. I know, I spent part of a bright, breezy day sitting on the wall with Chris, watching, through binoculars, the calving of the pond ice thirty yards away. It's amazing how fast that happens, once it starts, its six-inch edge deteriorating into vertical palisades, slumping off into the rippling wavelets of the pond surface. With the foreshortening of binoculars, it looks just like a glacier in an Alaskan nature film.

This was the earliest ice-out since we've lived here, according to our kitchen calendar. Chris marks down the significant occurrences in the natural year—notable weather, gardening details, the first migratory bird sightings—and the last week of March and the first two weeks or so of April are positively crammed with both climatology and ornithology. (The page for May is almost empty, with nothing but birthdays: by then the natural year is in place.) Notations get transferred to the next year's calendar, so we have accumulated a rough eight-year picture for this particular piece of hillside geography. Ice-out has come as late as April 20 (in 1982, when eighteen inches of snow fell on April 6), but in 1986 the pond was warm enough to swim in—people, not just dogs—on the twenty-ninth. Springtime being reliable only in its unreliability.

The returning birds pick their days (as do I). I have trouble paying enough attention to be a good bird-watcher, but in springtime, with whole new categories of bird showing up every day, there's not much choice. Chris, blessed with the specific quality of attention that I lack, keeps me up-to-date on local bird matters. She hears bird song, for instance, in a way I can't seem to manage. *Return of the Secaucus Seven* was filmed near our former home in northern New Hampshire; in it the background sound track, rather than the pictures, was the part that spoke to Chris of home. Oh, she said, those are *our* wood thrushes. Until then she hadn't realized that they had a regional accent (and didn't know how much she'd missed them).

I can't hear that accent, but then bird song rarely penetrates the gibber in my head anyway. When I try to listen to it my mind wanders off, usually into something like physiology. How *do* they make those sounds? It isn't a whistle, is it? (Birds can't exactly purse their lips.) It's song, all right, some kind of complex shout, or cry, air squeezed out of bird-sized lungs across bird-sized vocal cords. Little bitty muscles, doing work: bird labor, for which a certain amount of the energy budget must also be set aside. A single bird, flexing a bit of muscle and connective tissue smaller than a matchhead, filling the woods with sound. At sundown, the melting liquidity of the wood thrush's song—responsible, when I do manage to listen, for an untrustworthy sensation in the region of my own vocal cords—is also fueled by the conversion of glucose into adenosine triphosphate. From grasshopper meat, no doubt.

Thinking of such things gets in the way of hearing the song. To learn to listen better, I sit with Chris through summer sunsets, trying to pick out the last thrush's call of the day— which is impossibly backward, since you can't realize it was the last one until a quarter of an hour after you heard it. The quality of my attention falls away quickly, though, and between calls, between the very notes, I slip off into some other foolish speculation and miss the song. According to our friend Becky, what the wood thrush says is, "Here I am." Long pause. "Over here." Long pause. "Loving you." It is very peaceful, never mind the feeling it gives you at the back of the throat.

———

Mending harness, that's what farmers were supposed to do at times like these, at least in the books of my childhood. This cozy image of fireside craft lodged in my imagination: something neat and workmanlike to do, while barred from the out-of-doors where real work went on. I don't suppose there's all that much call for harness-mending skills anymore. Servicing machinery, rather. Our April weather finally turned warm enough for that, and I spent a compulsively satisfying afternoon changing the tractor oil and spark plugs, checking wear, getting everything cleaned and lubricated, the mower blades sharp. (The tractor does more mowing than hauling stone anyway, although the beginning of that particular chore is weeks away.) And, picking my days, I could get at least some of the outdoor work done, picking up winter trash and doing other spring chores.

Finally the weather holds dry and windy for forty-eight hours, and then I notice a significant amount of bird racket at dawn, always a good sign. Maybe the ground is dry enough to haul a load of stone. At noon I hitch up and head up the hill on the lane that ends the loop. The tumbled-down remains of old walls line both sides, but there are sizable gaps, one of which I began widening last fall, cannibalizing stones. I back the wagon into place, put down a loading plank, select the first stone of the day—the first stone of the year—and map out a pathway for managing it into the wagon.

The old wall is twenty feet from the road, and up a gentle sidehill slope. The stone I choose is a flat slab of gray-green granite, an irregular disk weighing maybe eighty pounds; I slide it off the wall onto its edge, keeping it balanced so I can roll rather than lift it down to the wagon's gangplank. Where the terrain won't let it roll, I walk it, rocking it from side to side, gaining a few inches with every teeter. As I tip it back and forth, the rock steps up onto its nearest low point and pivots—forward if I have the weight going in the right direction, backward if I've lost momentum. The weight of the stone chooses where it wants to swing next; my job is to keep tilting it so the way it chooses is the way I also choose—like a football lineman, attempting to control, or at least divert, my ponderous opponent.

"He's bigger than you, you'll just have to out-quick him," the football players say. I see what they mean. It takes little or no effort to hold the stone *in* balance; it takes a large effort to move it *to* a point of balance; it takes a much larger effort to stop and reverse its motion. Balance is everything; the earlier you react, the less effort you need to maintain control. The stones may not be as quick as professional football players, but they are quick enough—and the heavier the quicker, which is the scary thing. And their edges are scratchier.

Being quick on demand is a nervous and unfulfilling activity. Put some momentum with it, however—prior control, intent— and it becomes seductive. I love to trot up streambeds, leaping from stone to stone. A straight-line path is impossible; you have to swing back and forth like a hyperactive compass needle, vectoring your way upstream. You never quite capture your balance, and you don't want to; if you do, you stall, momentarily stuck on one rock. Your body weight becomes something you catch and toss with each foot, and you dance— searching for a workable rhythm, inventing a new beat every third or fourth step—as you go. When you really get it going, it's not like running so much as like working out with a light bag—using your feet instead of your hands.

Rolling rocks down to the wagon is a slower, upside-down version of that recreation.

If a stone can be lifted easily it is inconsequential, and fetching it is a small but tedious chore. If lifting it gives me pause, makes me figure out ahead of time where I'm going with it when I get it lifted, the task stops being tedious. If the stone is more than I can lift, it becomes a project, requiring pry-bars, rollers, the technology of moving heavy things—sports equipment for a game, the point of which is getting the most stone for the least effort. Big stones are more fun, making me try to figure out the physics.

Not that the selection of stones is in any way an orderly process: I probably choose them more by mood than anything else—at least until I have a specific hole to fill. If I'm all full of myself, I go after big ones, four or five to a wagonload; if I am just working to be outdoors, or because the uncompleted wall nags at me, I settle for smaller, less interesting stuff. There is also the sizable problem, on any given day, of getting started. It's as easy not to start stone work as it is not to start anything else. Bringing in a load of stone takes about twenty minutes and leaves me fairly filthy; laying up a load of stone takes an hour, or as long as I will give it—since, theoretically anyway, more time only makes the wall nicer. And other excuses. I try to work every day the weather allows, but don't quite get around to it. Once under way, though, I really enjoy it.

———

The idea that the investment of more time will make the wall nicer grows naturally out of the pursuit of tightness, of fit. The wall is by definition a loose structure, but the more tightly you can pull it together, the more satisfactory it's going to be. After a while you don't think much about the wall's size and shape because you're busy trying to tighten it up, fill all its holes. You stare, your head aswarm with the shapes of the holes you want to fill and the shapes of the stones available, looking for a match, and then for a better match. You *sort* stones endlessly, dreaming of the one that will sit most securely on what's below, most fully take up its allotted space. Stacking becomes obsessive. I find myself trying to get a better fit even when I'm loading stones into the wagon. But then, after I've been pruning trees I can no longer look at a tree for examining its limbs, searching for ones that need to go. After a session of stone work I see the world as a collection of gaps to be filled, my eye searching for shapes that will fill them. I see a barn on the horizon and automatically begin searching for a gap in the trees into which it would be a better fit, levitating it and rotating it in my imagination.

"There's a bed for every stone," says a wall-builder called the Kaiser, in Richard Conniff's *Irish Walls*. "You put it there and say, 'Get in it.'" When I pull a particularly well-fitting stone out of the old wall, I find myself imagining the pleasure of the original builder when he put it so snugly there. "Get in it," I hear him say.

Not that stone work holds an exclusive franchise in these satisfactions. In *House*, Tracy Kidder watches a thoughtful carpenter named Jim Locke build a staircase:

This is the most exacting moment on the stairs. Jim cuts, chisels, whispers precautions, and at last, he lowers the tread over the two bottom posts. Wood squeaks, birch against oak. "You couldn't get a razor blade in beside any of these posts, by God. How much? Five dollars? What's the statute of limitations? Tight for twenty years? Tight fits are what matter. Some people don't feel that way about life at all, but I know what quality feels like to me. What quality means to me is how tightly things fit together. Joints are the essence of it to me. . . . Usually, when you're done and there's a place where it's not quite perfect, you find a way to tighten it up. If you have a guilty conscience you do that. Sounds right anyway. By God that's close enough. . . ."

Joinery, it now occurs to me, must be the foundation of all craft. You put two things together to make something else, to accomplish some purpose; the better they fit, or work together, the greater the pleasure from the making. Stone, wood, glass, metal, mud, any material, any combination, it's the fitting together that turns work into pleasure, turns tedium into trance. Add to that list flesh (sex being work, in the physiological sense): the caressing hand pleasures more, and is more pleasured, the better it fits the curve it strokes. The better the curve fills it. I hadn't thought there was that much sexuality in stones.

_____

If I talk of stone work as if it is calmly and rationally done, will that make it so? Will putting the word on it help?

One of the standing files on my desk is labeled "Change or Die"; into it I throw clips and scribbled notes about the necessity for change for reasons of health, and schemes for the accomplishment of that change. They are fodder for the journalism by which I earn a living. Most but not all of the schemes take a physiological approach: diet, exercise, stress-reduction techniques, and other ways to resist the bodily ravages of aging. Sometimes it occurs to me that keeping a file folder and throwing notes into it is exactly the sort of behavior I need most to change. Filing away the need for change excuses me from changing: relax, it's taken care of, I have a file on that.

I have tried to describe leaving the city as a rational act, but at the time there was more than a little hysteria to it. (For me, anyway; I won't speak for Chris, a more ordered person.) It was less a moral or esthetic choice than simple burn-out, that dreadful combination of fatigue and despair. In my first job in New York, the man I replaced had turned over his desk to me personally. "This drawer is where I put the stuff that needs action but that I haven't yet figured out how to handle," he said. When I quit two years later, and repeated the routine with my replacement, I realized I hadn't managed to take a single thing out of that drawer, and in fact had added to its contents. That irreducible drawerful, the floodtide beating against my cubicle door, had become my personal nightmare of city life. I couldn't handle it, although I wasn't admitting it to myself as I left. I only dreamed of reducing the number of paper events in my life.

One of the things I had noticed when I first moved to the city was that the automatic elevators had a button labeled "close," implying that it operated the doors. Occasionally it seemed to do so, but that may have been an accident of timing; more often when you pushed the button, nothing happened. I always suspected that it was not hooked up to anything, that it was a fake, an anxiety reliever. Watch how we step into the car, whirl, and jab the button (two or three times for good measure): I'm here, let's *go*, get this thing moving. It is what I came to think of as the city disease, the urban scurry. Pushing against time. I hated it—and loved it, with a secret lust.

Someone should do a scientific study: does pushing the button lower the blood pressure (you've taken what action you can, it's in the hands of the elevator gods), or raise it (you're in a pocket of dead time, beyond your control)? One punches the button to get on to the next thing, whatever that is. Punching the button released a wave of hormones, I'm sure, to some yet uncharted hope-center of my brain or gut. Followed, I'm also sure, by a backwash of the biochemicals of despair—at the button's slowness in working, at my foolishness for trying to call up the present tense. Pressing the button was a waste of time, and not pressing the button was a waste of time. When I left the city I took the button with me, of course.

Earlier I spoke of seeking a more accurate alignment with the physical world. That lofty elocution implies a clearer goal than my daily life ever quite presents, and the more or less rational, methodical, even competent wall builder that I seem to be describing here is also a figment of my twitching imagination (which never quite thinks I'm actually doing what I'm supposed to be doing). Nevertheless, picking up a heavy stone does call up the present tense more effectively than pushing the button to close the elevator doors. Or at least that's my assumption. Sometimes it works, and sometimes it's only a different kind of desperation move, but it is never a paper transaction.

The sugar-makers will soon be taking down the sap buckets. Once you hear peepers, they say, sugaring is over for the year, which is why the last batch of sap is called the frog run. When I first heard of this concrete line of demarcation, I was charmed right out of my socks. And what signal, I asked, says that it is time to start sugaring? I never got a straight answer: you just hang the buckets, you know, when it's time. When you start getting consistent midday thaws. For the sap to run, you want a hard freeze at night, above-freezing temperatures during the day. If you don't get that kind of weather, you don't get a maple syrup crop. There are plenty of maples in western Massachusetts, but the local industry gets decent sugaring about one year out of three, and a really good year about one out of five, just about like any other kind of farming.

For several years I wrote the annual weather story for *Skiing* magazine. In the September issue, the magazine would run an article about why the previous winter had been a good one or a bad one for skiing, and what might be expected, in the way of snow cover, for the next season. This involved calling various climatologists, who would tell me in various complex ways that they really couldn't tell me why one year was different from another. The published piece would be useless generalization; weather is specifics, but you can't make a national magazine article out of that. Each year I scaled new heights of vagueness.

My crowning achievement in this silly enterprise came when someone told me about the circumpolar vortex, a meteorological term for the flow of cold air around the pole. The edges of this polar cap are scalloped, in effect, into lobes of colder, denser air that, in wintertime, extend its southward domain. It rotates west to east; the jet stream, the constant west-to-east flow of high-altitude air, traces its outline, influencing the course of storms. Low pressure wetness usually comes on the upswing between two lobes, howling northers on the downswing—the "Montreal Express" in New England, or, when things really get brutal, the "Alberta Clipper." The classic nor'easter comes when a lobe of the circumpolar vortex sits over New England with its eastern edge just off the coastline, and a moisture-laden low pressure area then slides up the coast and stalls. The counterclockwise circulation of the low pumps sea moisture into the lobe of cold air sitting over New England, making snow in winter, rain the rest of the year. The monster blizzards—1888, 1978—result.

Other commentators on the weather would talk of the jet stream; I, opting for the Latinate, would pull out the old circumpolar vortex. We were talking about the same things, but the circumpolar vortex supplied a larger pattern, an organization of the weather that helped my comprehension. In dead of winter the lobes of the circumpolar vortex extend well down into the temperate zones. The only relief comes with an anomaly, a deep upswing, as in our traditional January thaw. In stormy March, the edge of the circumpolar vortex is beginning to pull back through New England; the great energy of its heat exchange gives the region its legendary unreliable springtime weather. By April the show's about over—although, often as not, we'll get a "freak" foot of snow sometime in mid-April. See our kitchen calendar.

The violent weather has nothing to do with the hard freezes at night and thaws during day. This is a different pattern, the one that has to do with the angle of the planet, a more orderly progression. At this time of year I keep reviewing these two

patterns—the way one says one's beads, I suppose—to maintain my equanimity. (A song by the late Stan Rogers comes to
mind: "Sixty-five miles into town, and a winter's thirst to
drown, / A winter still with two months left to go.") I'm not
sure why it helps me to think about where the planet is in its
progression, and where the cap of polar air on top of that planet
is in *its* progression, but it does. The building of stone walls,
I notice, is also a laying down of patterns, enforcing order on
the fields, on the stones. Using stones to draw straight lines—
or curves, for that matter—on the face of nature, against its
chaos. Faced with raw nature, we go scurrying about in search
of a handhold, some kind of measuring device, for taking it
in. Meteorology will do. I'm okay as long as I can see the
weather as pressure gradients, clouds and vapors, great sweeping molecular embodiments. Events. Then I can stand it. It's
trying to accomplish something standing around in a breezy
thirty-six-degree drizzle—in the wrong clothes—that makes
me lose sight of the elegance of God's great patterns.

The evenings begin to stretch out; daylight saving time comes
along soon and gives us an artificial but nonetheless sweet new
hour of outdoor time in the evening. Our house is situated with
a view to the north and west, and as spring comes on, the
sunsets march out from behind the hillside, richening daily in
intensity. Connecticut Valley light, Chris calls it, although
we're fifteen miles from the river. (Or Maxfield Parrish light:
his studio was a hundred miles north, just on the other side
of the river.) The logical side of my brain tells me this is
nothing but an accident of the light rays, bouncing off particles
in space, working on rods and cones at the back of the eyeball,
but it is sufficient to pull me out the door. Moving me, however
haltingly, in the direction of a more sensory life.

Which, the older I get, the more I need. I am amused at how my appetites grow more, rather than less, sensory—in contradiction to the usual propaganda of youth. There's physiology for this, too, or so my file tells me. Age narrows the range of response, taking away the sensory highs and lows (just as it narrows the range of skeletal motion if one doesn't keep one's flesh stretched out to length). Age keeps trying to pull a layer of insulation between me and the world, making me want more brightness, vividness, for all my senses. I yearn for clean moves, sharp junctures, impeccable timings.

In late afternoon Chris joins me where I work on the wall. Cooperating in my efforts to keep my middle-aged senses stretched, she announces a special dinner to celebrate daylight saving time: fresh asparagus, a good red wine, candlelight, a little David Oistrakh. Every bit of it is glorious, and—now warm and cozy, suffused, joints gradually giving up the day's aches—I grow mildly drunk. I am sitting chin in hand, elbow on table, hip bones in chair, a collection of angles of propped-up bones making the armature on which the flesh is strung. On which I am strung. There, enveloping my skeleton, sits whatever it is that is me: soft tissue, the physiologist calls it, the stuff that "flesh-and-blood" refers to. Your skull can sit on someone's desk two hundred years from now, but it won't be you, it's just a mineral deposit, a tombstone. Bones as stones: you too can make a wall.

[4]

M A Y :

R H Y T H M I C S

There's rhythm enough to stone work if you can find it, a natural swing: stone snatched into the air, pivoted into position, deposited into place. Some days you have to feel around, hunting with limbs and joints, to find the timing. It teases you: the closer you come to getting it right, the easier the work will go. Somewhere, always just out of reach, there is the stone-work equivalent of hitting the sweet spot, that magic alignment of forces and masses that gives maximum result for minimum energy.

The sweet spot has to do with percussion (as in driving a golf ball, hitting a home run), and stone work is not ordinarily a percussive task. There is a rare but roughly analogous moment, though, when you plunk the stone down into a snug fit. Once in a while the stone lands solid, every knob and hollow making contact at the same time, no rocking into place, no searching out of equilibrium after the first contact of stone with stone. It's very satisfying. Striving for it, you eventually stop placing stones and begin dropping them the last half inch. Then they fall into place—or near enough to it—with a minor-grade percussive pleasure. The sound you want to hear is a small, soft clink, the signal that one unit is completed, releasing you to reach for the next. You want that sound to be singular; if it isn't, if the stone rattles into its spot, you have to wrestle it around a bit in search of a more solid seat. There's a wall-builder in the eastern part of the state who refuses to work if heavy machinery is operating nearby. He needs quiet, he says, to tell if the stones fit.

Some of this tossing of stones occurs naturally and spontaneously, as when you suddenly discover you don't want to lug the son of a bitch one inch further. Besides, if you keep placing stones instead of dropping them, your attention will eventually fail and you'll mash a finger. This happens not from the top—setting the stone down on yourself—but from the side: you swing it so it bumps into a stone already in place, using your fingertip as boat fender, a little fleshy pad to soften the impact of stone against stone. A mashed fingertip hurts about as sharply as any small physical injury you can do to yourself—and seems to get worse six hours or so later, in bed, when the blackening, bulbous mass starts throbbing as if to glow in the dark. Mashing fingertips quickly teaches you to drop stones into place.

So "throwing" stones onto your wall isn't entirely workman's slang. And because you do throw them, because you yank them off the earth (use your inertia to overcome theirs), and swing them toward their new site (momentum is easier than muscle), and drop them into place—and move your weight to them to pick them up, and set it to transport them, and move it away from them to go for the next—there is plenty of rhythm to be found in the task. Rhythm, after all, requires only a tap and a pause, a movement and that movement's landing. Or maybe a pause and then a tap: a *start* (the hard part), a move, and then a finish. And in between, there is all this roomy time in which to search for the less effortful way.

————

Steady rain, can't work on the wall, time for the spring inspection tour anyway. Getting all dolled up in rain gear makes me feel like a first-grader going off to school, but the downpour is as good an excuse as any to go fool around in the woods.

A spring inspection is actually a good idea, or feels that way. It seems only responsible to go check for damage— washouts, downed trees, and other winter havoc. Not that I'm going to be putting much of it right again. Inspecting the woods in the rain is perfectly satisfactory if you don't mind getting hit in the face with a wet branch every now and then. That is, going there in the rain doesn't seriously lessen the pleasure, it just removes the taint of doing it *for* pleasure.

In early May the foliage is still sparse enough to reveal the contour of the land, and that's trouble right there: when I can see the ground forms I start having grandiose ideas—to divert little streams, put a dam here and make a small pond, a footbridge over there, cut a road into this grove so I can bring the wagon in and get at those wonderful stones in the old fence-row on the back side. And gee, this is a nice part right here, why don't I just clean out this underbrush and make it into a nice little park, for summer strolling? And assorted other projects that I couldn't get done in two lifetimes.

I stifle that impulse, trying just to walk around and see how things are. As they are. To see if anything strange has developed. No, that's not right: to see how nothing strange has developed, even when there's damage; to see how dependably the same, after the winter, the woods always are. All I'm really doing is refreshing my memory of the part of the landscape hidden beneath the snow for the past months. Waterproof rationale thus in hand, I head out the back door and across the pasture and around the end of the pond, and up the hill past the abandoned sugar shack into . . . terrain. Nothing but terrain up here, and some wonderful trees, and a certain amount of wildlife: a universe of items I wish I knew the names of.

I don't know the history, either—of the fallen-down sugar hut, for instance, discernible now only as a lumpy green pile of punky wood-rot, marked by faint, unnaturally straight lines where there used to be boards. (But underneath the rot there is still some sound stone work, moss-grown foundations buried in soft, benign forest trash.) The sugar-shack wreckage, like the abandoned stone walls, gives these woods a human history, but I don't know its story. All that remains of its sugarbush— New England understatement for a maple grove—are a half-dozen monster trees a hundred yards apart, four feet or more in diameter and poking up high above the surrounding canopy. "Bush" seems comically inappropriate: each is a mighty botanical engine, eighty or more feet tall. In winter their broad limbs hold the snow, outlining them in white when all the smaller trees about them dissolve into the gray background; in spring they leaf out first, their access to the light expanding their growing season to match their disproportionate size. They absolutely dominate—pleasurably—this particular patch of land.

The sugar shack is partway up a steep hillside that is terraced with ledge and old logging roads, spotted with knolls, dissected by tumbling springtime brooks fated to dry up in another month or two. Over the first ridge there's a small ravine, a particularly cozy nook in the woods. Minor stone walls—natural ones— mark it off; on one side sits a glacial erratic, a great polished gray whale of an isolated boulder perched on top of mossy green bedrock strata pushing up from below. Muscular roots writhe over the rock surfaces in search of soil. So much stone, so much grinding and upthrusting violence, sounds rugged enough for the Rocky Mountains, but it's not: the moss and humus soften it like a goose-down comforter. The visual effect is Leatherstocking country, the romantic style of woods that N.C. Wyeth painted to illustrate James Fenimore Cooper—which were the illustrations that formed my childhood notion of what woods were supposed to be like. These woods are gentler than Wyeth's, though (and totally lacking in hostile savages—if you don't count July's deerflies). I go off into them every chance I get.

My assumption is that the enjoyment comes from the flora and fauna—that's what woods are, after all—but I notice that my route usually takes me from stone outcropping to stone outcropping, to places where biology is interrupted by geology. Something about the solidity of stone makes the woods more satisfactory, gives them a more comprehensible contour. Partly this is simple childishness, I suppose, a promise of fun: something to climb on, a gymnasium. But stone gives the woods visual relief. Underneath a thickening canopy, erupting through the cushion of leaf mold on the floor, rock makes a place in the woods to go to. One of these days I'm going to have to pay enough attention to see if the wildlife also feels that way about stone.

———

Paying attention is in fact the problem, walking in the woods. I go off on mental tangents, pursuing arguments, composing sentences—a minor-grade curse of writers, I suppose, too busy ordering thought to enjoy the surroundings. I get unplugged somehow from the sensory treasures around me, and lose the walk itself, the reason I went into the woods in the first place. This rainy morning I am determined not to let that happen, striding off wide-eyed, trying to see everything at once. It's pleasant enough duty: there is no softer light to see by, nor sweeter, richer air to breathe, than in foggy woods in the rain. The dogs certainly agree, suddenly electrified—ruffs rising, hard-pumping nasal passages going *whump whump whump* at all these big, moist particles of scent.

My own attention is visual, incorrigibly so. It is captured by a clump of birch, one spire of which has sagged off parallel to the ground, all wrong, violating the upright image of the species. That trunk is broken off, stub-ended, but from the stub has sprouted another spire that shoots straight up again. It's as if the tree spotted a little hole of light off to the side, stretched out a limb to get underneath it, then pointed a growing finger vertically toward the hole: virtually a new tree, created out of whole cloth by an opening in the canopy. Light as magnet, drawing a piece of tree to it. When light is let into these woods, birch is not what we usually get. The usual progression is ferns followed by blackberries and then various alders and other trash—what they call "popple" in New England. As I always rediscover after I've been taken with the clearing madness and have poked a new hole. But light is always working away, changing things, playing the forest the way a conductor plays a symphony orchestra, turning a hundred musicians into a single instrument.

That's light in botanical time, as opposed to geologic time. Geology—stone—seems impervious to light, but probably isn't, on some time scale or other. Some kinds of stone go notoriously rotten once they're exposed. Air and moisture do most of the damage, but I'll bet that light plays a part in these chemical transactions. It's easy to forget how powerful light is. Scientists, I've read, cross one laser beam with another, and at the juncture—where organized light piles up against organized light—stop atoms in their tracks. (And then photograph the atoms frozen there, capturing *their* light and slapping it onto paper.)

Meanwhile, on our time scale, stone gives light some nice stuff to work with: shadows, contours, surfaces that change appearance with the angle of the source. What gives a stone wall that nice, tight, skinned look is a regular consistency to the length of the shadow cast by each stone as it emerges from the plane of the wall onto the stones below. When you work on a wall you use the sun as a protractor, shadows slicing down from your mistakes. If the shadows are even, then nothing is sticking out too far and the alignment is right. There's nothing to pull your eye away from the skin—the wallness—of the structure. The way natural stone keeps pulling my attention away from the woods.

————

Some of that attention also necessarily turns to the placement of the soles of my rubber boots, lest I get dumped on some other part of my rain gear. Walking in the rain is less pleasurable than it ought to be: muddy footing destroys the rhythm, turning the walk into some kind of risk game, jerking my weight around. It makes me realize how desperately one wants a decent rhythm in walking, in building stone walls, in trotting up stream beds, in any physical movement at all. It's an appetite that never quite gets sated. I don't dance anymore—out of stodgy inhibition, I suppose—and I miss it. I swim and run instead, faddishly, in programmatic exercise for the middle-aged. I no longer do it out of concern for my cardiovascular system so much as the need to burn off a little energy in long, gentle, rhythmic effort. Quiets the mind. Rhythm definitely soothes

(rock-a-bye baby); it also haunts, its presence organizing the
world, its absence, when I need it, throwing all into chaos.

I haven't tried working on the wall to music, but I've done
the playful physical work of athletics that way. It makes me
grin. I'll be grinding along, beginning to sag with fatigue, when
some funky old favorite comes along on the tape, and I find
myself automatically putting a little more effort into the work
again, gently pulled up to another level. Without music I tend
to forget that it is possible to enjoy the effortful part of exercise.

For a long time I resisted working out to music, objecting
to the wires in my ears. Then I tried it, and quickly saw what
dancers have always known, how music illuminates physical
motion. It gives a stable base, a kind of gravity of time from
which to act. The biomechanists say that initiation of movement
is the hard part, the part that takes the most energy. (Leave
a light bulb on and it'll last for years; turning it on and off is
what burns it out.) More neural signalling is required to start
a move than to keep it going. Rhythm relieves you of that
effort, organizing your effectors. The beat drops markers into
the motion, making its constituent parts come clear. The great
distance runners say the most important skill is learning to
relax while they run—which is surely connected, in some way
I'll never experience, to the way jazz musicians work with all
that roomy material between the beats.

Sometimes there's more difficulty in finishing moves than in
starting them. I first ran across this principle in downhill skiing,
where great instructional emphasis is placed on completing
one turn in order to get the next one started right. This didn't
make a whole lot of sense to me: you have to stop turning in
one direction if you're going to start turning in the other, don't
you? How could you do otherwise? I flailed and flummoxed my
way through a lot of awkward moments before the significance

of the advice sank in. Finishing is a positive act. A ski turn carried to its logical physical conclusion ends in an edge-set that makes a stable platform from which to start the next turn. "Finished" means your weight is in the right place, your body and skis prepared for whatever comes next. Without it, you're in trouble. You have no "timing."

It's the same in any sport, using any sports equipment, in dance, in stone work or any other movement. Any performance. (It is why letting stones drop percussively onto the wall is satisfying.) Only when moves become linked, serialized, automatic—rhythmical—can you see the lovely contradiction: taking time to finish one move gives you more time for the next.

Sometimes I have trouble initiating another day's work on my wall, sometimes I have trouble knowing when to quit. It's the skin on a wall—the finish—that is the signature: a level of trueness that says this piece of work is done.

It's a heavy, steady rain, now and then turning to tiny, bouncy balls of sleet as the atmosphere plays back and forth across the freezing point. This is our traditional spring storm, which can come as a couple of feet of snow instead of six inches of rain. It beats down the mosses and ferns that make up the forest floor (inviting you, in drier weather, to lie down), beats down the greenness that is starting over again, everywhere, after the winter crush. Before long there will be efts—tiny, sluggish, orange salamanders—in the path, and newts in the pond. I think that's what they're called. I don't know the proper names for all these things, and a pang of guilt whispers in my mind: names are words, and not to know them is to play hookey from my line of work. But then my attendance record has never been all that good anyway.

So *attend*, I tell myself, stepping up close to look at a beech tree's bark, trying to focus in, find some handhold for my attention. Beech bark looks like elephant skin, a smooth gray membrane except where it turns corners and gets wrinkled and baggy. Branches make stretch marks above and below the juncture with the trunk; where they're broken off, they leave graphic "eyes," surrounded by darker wrinkles above and below, like painted-on eyeliner, Arab kohl. The tree trunks in a beech grove thus are full of staring eyes—an effect that was not lost on the Disney studios.

Birch bark, on the other hand, is less superficially gorgeous, for all its stark whiteness, so vivid against dark woods. Up close, though, it's a light show, the white translucently overlaid with silver, old gold, yellows, rose, matte gray, layers of fungi. Birch bark is so gloriously complicated, up close, that it is a barrier to observation: I try to look at it as if to draw it, paying the hardest attention I can to its detail, but its profligacy overpowers the brain.

The biologist will stake out the woods square meter by square meter, and in any one of those blocks may find a career (or a lifetime's entertainment, same thing). Good idea: the woods all at once swarm me almost to boredom, forcing me to grab for details. Back when the snow was beginning to go, I kept having the urge to ski over and see if something was hiding in the conical depression around each tree's base. Nothing there but more tree, of course. More physics going on: the dark trunk absorbs enough of the sun's heat to melt out an inverted cone in the snow-cover, dotting the surface of the snow with giant ant-lion dens, each with a stem—a tree trunk—sticking up out of it. Tree as heat sink. Not to mention physiology: my botanist daughter (who does know the names of things) tells me that the chemical processes of photosynthesis also cause trees to run a daily temperature. And their trunks are larger in diameter in the daytime—when they are pumping sap—than at night. Inhale, exhale.

Annual rhythms are spelled out so clearly in tree rings that scientists use them to link drought cycles with sunspot activities. If our microscopes get fine enough, I suppose, we'll find a way to read daily rhythms as well (if we can figure out where to take the reading, where to insert the wedge of inquiry). Science seems quite taken, lately, with stripes, not only in tree rings but in rocks from Australian lakebeds, on seabottoms alongside the Atlantic Rift: stripes that spell out the flip-flop of the magnetic poles, the stately cruise of continental drift. Actually, the stripes the scientists read these days are more likely in computer print-outs, where numerical values bunch and then spread apart. A rhythm being a stripe in time: glory be to God for stripèd things.

The power of the rain raises a wave of alarm at the erosion so clearly taking place; I have the panicky impulse to start throwing up bulwarks against the loss of topsoil. In the path, the rain is exposing little loops of rootlets, miniature cables across a miniature streambed. Debris collects, making the cable thicker, building up a little dike; when the waters slow, the sediment falls out, forming a paddy, a tiny terrace. The newly exposed root stubble calls up the term "biomass" in my head—all that wonderful once and future live stuff, which erosion is busily tearing up, carrying off.

Then I let myself off the hook: it's just a pipsqueak local mountain coming down, changing its shape, a process that is going to go on anyway, one way or another. To fight it in these woods is just to nudge the time scale infinitesimally in the direction of my personal desires. Yes, the erosion is worst in the old logging roads, where disruptive man has accelerated the pace of change. But that's all it is, a change in the pace. Underneath, it all comes to bedrock anyway—which is also coming down, but on another, entirely less alarming time scale.

Why do I always find something to worry about on these walks, some project I ought to be undertaking? Something up here on the hill that just needs *managing*, you know? I go for a walk to see the woods, and end up seeing flaws: another failure of attention. Somehow I'm trying to pay attention to the walk in exactly the wrong way, in a way that shuts off experiencing it. That's what I want to cure myself of: the disease that has me wondering, when I finish a walk, how it would have been up there in the woods, in the rain, if I'd only been paying attention.

The rain dwindled off that night, and over the next day or two the summer began to settle in in earnest. Bringing, in mid-May, the blackflies. They intensify with the humidity, becoming noticeably peskier on those still, muggy days when the sun is beginning to develop real power. I'll start work on the wall with the best of intentions, but before long sweat is running into my eyes and blackflies are bouncing back and forth between my face and the inner surface of my eyeglasses, which makes me crazy. No sooner do I get a heavy stone hefted than I drop it to swat a biting fly. After fifteen minutes or so of this I'll realize the soft, whining noise I keep hearing is coming from myself, and I throw up my hands and quit—sometimes deciding to do so while already on a dead run for the pond. After all, there's no time constraint on this project. It's not as if I have to get the goddamned wall built to keep the cows in.

We don't have the chiggers I knew in the Southwest, and ticks are locally rare, but of the remaining universe of blood-sucking insects, we are supplied with blackflies, mosquitoes, and deerflies. They arrive not quite serially: blackflies are the ones that quietly swarm your head in early summer; mosquitoes peck at your ankles, mostly at evening or in the shade, all summer long; whizzing, dive-bombing deerflies enrage you from June to mid-August, increasing when the wind is out of the south, mercifully decreasing with cooler, drier air from the north. Deerflies, like dogs, love any kind of milling action; the more frantically you slap at them the more excited they become. Flailing away at one of them always seems to call up two or three more as reinforcements.

I do not like it that biting flies make me so crazy. I struggle to reach a calmer accommodation, but I fail. The first few blackfly bites of the year itch from the site of the bite—usually a bulging major vein on the wrist or back of the hand—all the way up to the armpit and beyond, the torment submerging deeper into the flesh the further it gets from ground zero. The itch, they say, is caused by a tenderizing enzyme in the fly's saliva; the first injection of the year achieves a biochemical reaction that makes the very walls of the blood vessels seem to itch as the stuff is pumped on toward the heart. In any event, it's too deep to scratch.

The bite subsides in a couple of hours, and leaves not an ill effect but a benign one: each subsequent bite seems to itch a little less, and by the time the blackflies begin to die off, I'm more or less immune anyway. I must also admit that our local deerfly is a relatively innocuous creature, at least in comparison to its New Hampshire cousin, which likes to tear off a chunk of flesh, chew it up, and spit it back into the wound as a catalyst for the coming operation. They tell me that Cape Cod's infamous greenheads (underpublicized, like the shark in *Jaws*) are worse.

There is a profound philosophical implication, I'm sure, to the triangular relationship between biting fly, man, and nice places out-of-doors, but the bugs keep me too busy cursing to think about it. Dry, breezy days are fine, but to try to work outdoors in early summer when one of those dismal low-pressure sumps has settled in is to be driven to despair by the bugs. They wear you to a frazzle. It isn't the bites, or avoiding the bites, that exhausts you, it's the pace at which they make you work. And they destroy all hope of rhythm, of course.

When Chris and I tap our feet to music, our footfalls don't match up. We hear the same music but do not tap to the same beat (another reason for giving up dancing). One of us is surely early, or late, but I can't tell which, I only know I'm on the beat I hear. Perhaps we don't hear the same music after all, now that I think of it. Chris tends to hear harmonies, I hear only the melodic line. Why does that seem to me a sexually appropriate division of responsibilities?

Music in the henhouse makes more eggs, in the dairy barn, more milk. I've puzzled over dogs' rhythms. It has always disappointed me that animals don't tap their feet. (Never mind the ponderous circus horses and elephants; they're even further off the beat than I am.) There's very little that dogs do that doesn't have rhythm to it, from the way they trot to their diurnal cycles, but they've never quite taken their rhythmicity that next, human step. Maybe that's the essential division between man and animals: building rhythms into strings long enough to be worth pursuing. Inventing music.

There are a couple of wall-builders in New Hampshire who work to music—classical in the mornings, jazz in the afternoons (and no rock and roll: "Can't handle hard rock with rock work," one of them says). The music, they claim, finds its way into the walls. It don't mean a thing if it ain't got that swing.

SUMMER

PART II

[5]

J U N E :
J O C K
R O C K S

About the time summer was getting fully under way, our friend
Hans decided to put in a retaining wall, and hired a stonemason
to help him. I volunteered as work crew in exchange for wall-
building lessons. I was expecting the stonemason to be some
grizzled old-timer, with maybe a little tobacco juice on his
chin; he turned out to be a tall, slim, good-looking woman in
her mid-thirties named Linda Mason ("Yes, that's actually my
name"), with a mane of flaming red hair and a no-nonsense
approach to stone work. Among other things.

"Slim" does not convey her solid trimness: she handled most
stones more easily than I did, and I outweighed her by fifty
pounds. (The first time I saw her lift a large stone, I squelched
a bewildered impulse to rush to help. I didn't have that impulse,
I noticed, when Hans lifted a stone. At least not unless the
stone was considerably larger.) Except for a blackened fingernail or two, she bore no physical clues to her craft. I asked
her what she did for relaxation, when she wasn't building walls.

"Oh," she said, "I like to knit, sew, do crochet. Take my car apart. That kind of thing."

A truckload of Goshen stone had been dumped in Hans's front yard. We would fetch stones from the pile until we had a reasonable assortment spread around the foot of the retaining wall, then start puzzling out which went next. For footings, Linda wanted only a single layer of three- to four-inch-thick stones, flat on the upper surface to give a tablelike foundation on which to erect the aboveground part of the wall. Goshen stone is soft, wafery stuff, one piece looking pretty much like the next; it forces you to work small, in chunks that aren't much larger than, and look as stackable as, books. But aren't. The wall that results is extremely neat, at the cost of a lot more fussiness with fit than when you're working with field stone. Goshen stone goes slowly. I didn't like working with it much, and was gratified to learn that Linda, too, preferred ordinary field stone.

Essentially, she told us to put two stones on one and one stone on two, and then moved off to another part of the wall to smoke cigarettes and stack stones of her own. She would wander back to check our work from time to time, keeping us in line and on track. Once I left a stone unstable, rocking on a high spot. She spotted it immediately. "I don't like that and neither do you," she said, pulling it down, turning it over, giving its underside a couple of good whacks with hammer and chisel, and plopping it back firmly and securely in its place. "See?" she said, as she walked away. "You get total control."

Trailing words as she wandered off was Linda's trademark— a manifestation, I think, of the staring process, of all that time spent trying to make vague shapes fit together in the mind. Memorizing holes, as one wall-builder describes it. A costume party was coming up, and Hans asked her what she was going

to wear. "I don't know. Last year I went as Tina Turner. Maybe
I'll go as a cowgirl," she said, and drifted off. She was ten
feet away when I heard her add, under her voice, "I've already
got the horse."

As summer wore on and my own wall nagged at me, my
participation dwindled. Linda and Hans finished the front steps
and got half the rest of the wall done, then Hans ran out of
stone and spare cash at about the same time. He wouldn't
resume the project until the next spring. When he did, he
ordered another load of stone and then, too busy to fool with
it himself, hired a three-man crew to finish his wall. They were
very fast, he told me, picking up whichever stone was nearest
to hand and chopping it with masonry tools to fit where they
wanted it to go. Total control. They finished the job in one
working day. It's very neat.

From *Irish Walls*: "One local man so admired the towering wall
at Moran's place that he went out with his dog and gazed at it
for a half-hour at a time, until one day the dog (gone mad with
boredom) got away from him and was killed (doubtless by a
driver who was looking at the wall instead of the road)."

Back at home, dismantling the old wall, I began from time to
time to get a ghostly feeling that I might be seeing the stones
through the eyes of the original builder, seeing as he (or she?)
must have seen them. The way some stones had been placed
just made more sense than others. I began to notice places
where my predecessor had done a good job, and where not.

I still couldn't say what it was that I was seeing. Working
with stones holds you at the level of the absolutely specific;
generalizations are beside the point. You are solving a puzzle
with no rules—except for the one about two on one and one

on two, which you can seldom follow literally. That's why the books about stone work are frustrating: words don't work. General discussion about how random shapes might go together is no help at all when you're kneeling in front of a wall, about to pick up a heavy stone.

That may also be why it's difficult to talk about stone work, particularly with men. Casual talk among males relies heavily on the names of things—two-by-fours, piston displacements, the right kind of paint. There aren't that many names for stones. A stone that extends through the width of the wall, helping to tie both faces together, is a "tie-stone," or "thrufter." "Capstone" is self-explanatory (and a little precious on the tongue, now that I think of it). "Stack bond" refers to insufficient overlap between stones, leaving vertical joints or gaps (like "type rivers" in typography), but I wouldn't know how to use it in a sentence. That's about all the nomenclature I've been able to lay my hands on. Not much fuel there for a conversation.

Becky, who supplied the words to the wood thrush's call, had also done some wall building, and she and I could talk easily of the satisfactions of lifting heavy things into place, of seeing the landscape take a new shape. Males find that kind of talk a little fishy. Outdoor projects that don't involve at least a backhoe don't seem to merit talking about—unless you hurt yourself or uncover other comic possibilities in the occasion. If the subject of stone walls came up with a male friend, the talk would swerve almost immediately into granites and schists (about which I knew nothing and, worse, found it impossible to become interested), or the identity of a stonemason who'd done a nice chimney over in the next town. Linda Mason would admit that she enjoyed the work, sometimes even enthusiastically, but then would shy away from the subject. Doesn't do to talk about it, says the white hunter in the Hemingway short story. Talk it all away, you know.

Work is to be complained about, everybody knows that. (If it were fun, someone would surely take it away from us.) At a large social gathering I overheard the public violation of this convention, by a man whose main occupation was dentistry but who was building his own house. The weather had been glorious, and he had spent a rapturous Saturday outdoors, carrying clapboards from his pickup truck to his house and nailing them in place. "People would pay money for the privilege of doing that," he was saying, sunburned face aglow. He should float this proposition by a professional siding-installer, I think. It reminded me sharply that my wall was a personal indulgence, worked on in fair weather, at as slow a pace as I chose. It was work only in the physiological sense. (Physiologically speaking, so is lifting a glass of champagne to the lips.) In any other terms—moral, ethical, practical—it was an entertainment: play, not work.

So I tried to keep mum, but didn't always succeed, which meant that people kept telling me—the only polite response— about walls. Everyone had a favorite wall I should go see, knew a waller I must talk to. I wanted to watch more real wall-builders at work, but had no idea what I could talk to them about. I'd had trouble phrasing questions to Linda. You can't sensibly talk about the shapes of holes. And when I went to look at real stone work—old bridge abutments, for example, from before the days of stressed concrete, made of five-ton behemoths stacked dead level thirty feet off the ground—I was just stupefied. Stupefaction wasn't useful. I still found myself unable to study stone work to any result. Couldn't get my mind on it. I didn't want to look at more walls, I wanted to stay home and work on my own. Stop confusing me with the facts.

Settling a good-sized stone into the wagon, it occurs to me that this one came along fairly easily, that I'd done a reasonably efficient job of getting it. Only one stupid slip (and a minor whack on the shin). I give myself an A-. Larry Bird would do it with no slips at all, I reckon: A+; Greg Louganis would slip the rock down the slope and into the wagon like water flowing. That is, it is an athletic task, and like a proper jock, I try to improve at it, concentrating harder, anticipating more, attempting to reduce the effort while achieving the same result—and other principles of athletics, applied to fetching rocks. As the day wears on and I become fatigued, I feel myself as a hinged creature, divided at the waist into two large halves, hinged again, secondarily, at knees and elbows, and then again at ankles and wrists. I operate myself by pulling on levers across hinges. Muscles can't do anything but contract. When I push the stone up the plank, it is by contracting muscles, which pull on tendons, which cross the hinges of my joints and attach to my bones; the bones push the stone. What kind of physics is this, that pushes by pulling?

As the racing car enters a curve, the driver must wait for it to take a set before serious cornering can begin: the mass of the car must be settled down on its chassis, the flexibility of its suspension taken up, before the driver begins to get accurate information about how securely the tires are biting. The first stone of the day usually reminds me of this. I grab at it too casually, not really ready, and it simply brushes me off. Oh yeah, I think, *heavy*. I get a better placement for my feet, find a decent grip, and apply force more slowly. The set traverses my body segment by segment: muscles and tendons are pulled taut, the joints loaded sufficiently to get all the parts located, the physical slack taken out. Only then am I ready to move the stone—reassured that, among other things, I can take up the load without hurting something. Once again I am trying to learn to stop snatching at things, yanking and jostling them into place, depending on momentum and raw strength to do the job. I try to remember to circle each move before I make it, finding where, for a hinged creature, the leverage lies.

And then take a set. Applying force pulls tight the link between the grip of my feet on the ground and the grip of my hands on the rock; force transforms my body into a fleshly loop, replacing, as I lift, the linkage of stone to earth. Force turns me into a small crane. As a machine my capacity isn't great, but my flexibility and portability are exceptional. It's easy enough to set me up and take me down again, I just can't handle much weight.

Circling the move is the good advice of my friend Willy, who worked for a while, in his schooldays, with a truly accomplished forester. Charlie Gray was his name, an ancient and tiny slip of a man who seemed capable of miracles. Willy describes how Charlie would walk around a tree, spending silent minutes smoking his pipe, studying what he called the muscle of the bole. Then he'd fell it, bringing it down cleanly in a twenty-foot gap. He rarely missed; if he did, and ended up with a tangled mass of wood, he'd walk around that for a while too, then pick up just the right tool and give the problem a lick in just the right spot, and it would pop loose, solved. How was it, Willy would wonder, that this miniature woodsman had so much more leverage than everyone else?

When I told Linda Mason that I was volunteering to help with Hans's wall, she said, "You trying to get built up?" No, I quickly insisted, I only wanted to learn wall-building. I probably also winced: I hadn't heard that term since college, and associated it only with a particularly obnoxious type of cretin who lifted weights, I thought, just to look more muscular. Unmuscular myself, I was deeply suspicious of such behavior. There was one weight-lifter I knew personally from gym class; he had a hernia, and I remember watching him lie down on the floor of the locker-room to cinch his truss into place before disappearing into the weight room. It seemed like madness to me. Thirty years later—a couple of years before I met Linda Mason—I had selected my own personally satisfactory form of madness, and in the process had become a cretin myself.

I was trying to improve as an athlete, at a more or less inappropriate age, and the rate of gain was beginning to slow. According to the scientists, the objective components of athletic performance are speed, endurance, and strength. Speed is pretty much fixed, genetic; you can't do much with it. To continue to improve—the reigning obsession in athletics—you work on stamina and strength, both of which are readily and demonstrably trainable. In the beginning, I was convinced that endurance was the more interesting part of the equation; when that curve of improvement began to sag, I swallowed the prejudices of my college days and began training to increase strength. By lifting weights. It was a revelation.

I didn't add much bulk—I didn't work hard enough at it for that—but I did get a little stronger, and along the way I stopped thinking of weight-lifters as cretins. I had not considered lifting weights to have much to do with athletics, and to the extent that it did, I thought it was athletics reduced to the lowest common denominator: the simplest physical task available in the category of using the body to accomplish work. Athletics, I thought, deserved to be a little more sophisticated than that. The first surprise, then, was that weight-lifting was as complex and intriguing as any other athletic enterprise I'd ever attempted.

Lifting weights also gives you a cram course in the mechanical principles of the body. It requires that you isolate muscle groups and work them individually; as you work programmatically through the musculature, each new skeletal motion becomes for a time a separate small environment, with its own attachment points, available leverages, ranges of motion. What this gives you, in addition to tired muscles, is a detailed explication of the anatomy. To work with weights is, by definition, to deal with overload, with excess, and the excess teaches you new and different ways of working. You learn to ease weights into motion, to take small gains and consolidate them, to put power into brief bursts and to rest in between. That is, lifting weights doesn't just make you grossly stronger, it also sharpens your skill at using your body to generate force. I found this powerfully satisfying, in ways I can't entirely explain.

At bottom, the best part of weight-lifting for me was its own strange pleasure. Like most athletic endeavors, it began as drudgery. As I became accustomed to the style of the work, however, a sweet sensuality began to intermingle with the sweat and fatigue. It is curiously satisfying to have a concrete source of physical resistance, and then to overcome it, perhaps just in reaction to the vagueness of our push-button, power-assisted modern life. I'm not sure I want to think about this too much, but I notice that people also get a lot of satisfaction out of smashing tennis balls back over the net, the harder the better. Unleashing force—particularly controlled force, released harmlessly—seems to answer some fairly deep need.

Stone work is mostly weight-lifting—weight-moving, anyway—and I suppose I have a vested interest. I wouldn't have started wall-building if I hadn't already determined, perhaps on some preconscious level, that moving heavy things around for fun was suited to my nature. As it turns out, there is much less pure lifting to stone work—in the grunting sense of raising large weights into place—than I'd expected. There is no end, though, to the moving around of small stuff: easing thirty-pound stones, two-handed stones, over the lip of the wagon, sliding them out onto the ground at the wall site, heaving them into place. Lifting them three inches, rotating them half a turn, and then plunking them back into place. Messing around with small to medium weights.

Thinking about all this makes me realize that stone work is a mixture of craft and athletics. I didn't know that when I got into it, but—also at some more or less unconscious level— I'm sure that's why I took it up. When it's not going well, I fear I'll never really be good enough at either. The coach in me says that what I have to do is get in good enough shape— in the athletic sense—to keep at it long enough, consistently enough, to master the craft part: suck it up, stick it out, in the best jock tradition. But then in matters of self-discipline, Coach and I don't always see eye to eye.

Anyway, there's a part of stone work that is physical in the sense of the laws of physics (which is the craft part), and a part of it that is physical in the sense of physiology (the athletic part). When one part of it gets frustrating, the plan is to try paying attention to the other. This sometimes works.

———

When I speak of getting pleasure from the lifting of weight, I don't mean to imply that work is not drudgery. It's required to be: effort *hurts*, everyone knows that. I'm as big a sucker as anybody for the dream of the sweet life—the one they show

on TV, with a hammock and a beer, feet up, not a muscle cell
firing, giddy inhabitant of an effortless world. I love the way
we con ourselves that release from toil would be paradise on
earth, and then frantically boil off energy inventing electric
can-openers and automatic transmissions. We have these anat-
omies, muscles and minds, and we will by golly use them—
dreaming, all the while, of not having to anymore. Weird.

Drudgery has more to do with will than with effort, for me:
willing myself to work, keeping at it after the effort has become tedious or painful. I'm sure that what made the dentist-
carpenter's day so rapturous was doing the work not to pay the
bills or even to finish the house but to do the work. Getting
beyond reasons, to the work itself. The work was doing the
dentist, so to speak. This is not drudgery.

I have my own complaints about work. The way I get my
living consists, in the physiological sense of work, of sitting
at a machine and manipulating bits of light. Not exactly heavy
lifting. In fact the bits of light I look at and the keys I touch
with my fingertips are the only parts of the act that significantly
connect with the physical world. The distance between those
acts and anything concrete is considerable: the bits form the
letters which form the words which represent the sounds by
which we originally transmitted all thought. Not as many layers
of abstraction, perhaps, as when there's a weather map on the
TV screen, but enough. The writer's workplace is inside the
head. Or some other suitable metaphor for wherever it is that
thought actually takes place.

When it's going well, when it holds me and my attention to
it—when the work is doing me—I get to spend time in a
minor-league heaven: *there's* the paradise on earth. The better
the work goes, the deeper I get into the problem, the stiller I
get. I enter the writer's version of the computer-hacker's trance,

insulated from all external stimuli including even the messages
from my muscles and joints telling me for God's sake to move
around a little bit now and then. When the solution to a difficult
problem begins to come, I even strike the keys more softly,
not wanting to jar loose the thought.

Unfortunately, I can't stay in that delicious place. Attention
fades, and I have to will myself back to concentration. Then
I cross over from paradise into a pipsqueak hell, of jittery
nervous irritation, of whining demands from the body, of fatigue
on its way to depression. It becomes work, and I complain
about it. Writers are world-class complainers.*

Or maybe it's fortunate that I can't stay there, shriveling
into human concrete. Dutifully (willfully) I stay at the keys—
at "work"—long after I've stopped transmitting anything like
coherent thought. I am convinced that the guy in my head is
in control of this process, but the guy in my body—where the
sensors are located—has been flipping off lights and unplug-
ging circuits for several minutes now. The head is an airless,
stuffy place to work, and after a while the anatomy feels compelled to stagger up and throw open a window.

So I must learn, when I've fogged out at my desk, to go get
some kind of sensory reconnection with the physical world.
Preferably outside (my house as well as my head). Stone work
is a fairly vivid way of working the sensory apparatus. When
I can remember to do this—walk away from work-turned-
drudgery, reconnect with the sensations of the world—I also
remember that I am embarrassingly lucky to be able to do so.

---

*A few years ago Jonathan Raban published a fine book about sailing
around the British Isles, and Paul Theroux published an equally fine
one about walking around them. Each book acknowledges an encounter
with the other writer while in the field. During this encounter, each
writer assured the other that his own book was going wretchedly.

Or I remember it for a few minutes, anyway, until I get to worrying about something else.

But that's the thing about stone work: it spits you back in again. When I flee my desk, my intention is to put its problems completely and deliberately aside, go pay serious attention to the air, light, sun, sounds. After all, I remind myself, I'm trying to lead a more sensory life. But before long the problem that stalled me has floated up again, and I discover fresh new mental purchase on it. I resist this idea as excessively romantic—and a bloody cliché—but it's true: the busier my hands are somewhere else, the better I work in my head. I pay better attention to my work when I can think about it in a freely ranging way, outside the strictures of language and sentence structure. When I can let subjects come and go of their own accord (without my willing them). Unfortunately, that's not the part that gets me a living. Oh, I have my complaints about work, all right.

Anyway, stone work does not demand a lot of thought. After the first few minutes—remembering how to do it—you get to think about any damned thing you want. Some other part of your attention starts taking care of selection and alignment of stones, of the mechanical principles of moving weight, and your mind is set free as a colt turned out to pasture. Personally, I find that using the other part of my attention—the part that knows how to stack stones—is a powerful restorative. But that's stacking stones, not thinking about stacking stones, and particularly not thinking in words about stacking stones.

———

At dawn the bird chatter is sufficient to draw me out the door. (Just checking the weather, I tell myself, explaining my underwear.) The sky is mostly clear, but changing; I count five distinct categories of cloud, in five separate planes: five separate textures and structures, their variety demonstrating the great dimension of the atmosphere. To see more sky, I walk out from under the maples, and suddenly feel like the match-book in the corner of the photograph, placed there to indicate scale. I usually think of the air as a placid and uniform ocean, but here's a life-sized, full-color, working model, laying out today's vast range of currents, densities, changes of temper-ature. On some giant scale or other it is always turbulent, even when it looks and feels as perfectly still as this morning does.

Also quiet, for all the birdly enthusiasm. Farm lot sounds come drifting up from the valley, clearly distinct from the racket in the trees. Desultory, distant barking, likewise separate, which our dogs monitor but choose not to answer. There's a lot of space between these sounds. The whine of tires. At the bottom of the hill there's a moderately busy rural two-lane, which follows a local creek for a mile or two and then snakes back uphill to a small town (population 1,500, mostly scattered up similar valleys). Beyond the town there's a small lake, where flocks of Canada geese settle in for a visit each spring and fall. When in residence, they will startle up from time to time and make a low-level reconnaissance flight around the valley. Their honking bounces around the hills so crazily that you keep looking for them in the wrong place. The valley makes a catch-basin for sound.

With, as yet this morning, no chainsaws, making it a rare daylight moment indeed. (The curse of the two-cycle engine, a friend always mutters.) In warm weather, day or night, we're also likely to hear a motorcyle or two, revving to unimaginable r.p.m., shifting, revving again, drifting off in the distance. The sound waves make bank-shots off the far slopes, the war-bling revs also demonstrating atmospheric currents, densities, temperatures. Not exactly an organ in a cathedral, but it's a noise I can live with.

The farm lots send smells as well as sounds, attenuated over the distance but still pungent enough to make the dogs wistful. In *Adam's Task,* Vicki Hearne points out that dogs see about as we see, but discount much of that; what they believe is what they smell, and their noses are to ours "as a map of the surface of our brains is to a map of the surface of an egg." I sniff the still air myself and get only hints. With my vision-dominated imagination I picture those cavernous canine olfactories, the air currents swirling through them, seeking out receptor sites for, oh, manure, methane, milk, the gasses off grain and grasses growing. Frogs' breath, pond froth, maple vapors, all venting, all putting out molecules into the morning for dogs to smell. Giving them some utterly different picture of the world.

Aha, that's it, a valleyful of molecules this morning. Up close, vivid as an oil painting, but across the way a watercolor wash, the edges soft, colors muted. Too much diffraction between here and there. And I am left trying to figure out how, with all the bird racket and clamor from the valley, the view is so entirely peaceful. How can this be? What is the physics of this? How *did* that little woodsman get all that leverage?

[6]

SOLSTICE:

ALIGNMENTS

People who leave New England say they miss the seasons: springtime's renewal, autumn's sweet sad glories, even the austere beauties of winter. Fine, sure, but let's not kid around, it's summertime, high summer, that's the season, isn't it? The high point of the year, before which all is glowing anticipation, after which all is tinged with regret, nostalgia? We've known that—in our bones—since school days, haven't we? (Isn't that what they were telling us by institutionalizing the Summer Vacation?) I have tried to sell myself the other seasons—by way of getting through them, in their unpleasanter manifestations—but at the bottom of my heart there's never been any doubt about summer. Therefore, I pay attention when the solstice comes around. I find some way, privately, to acknowledge it. I don't paint my arse blue, but hell, it's the longest day of the year, after all. You *have* to love it, if you like days.

The building of walls is not all that goes on around here; among other projects I had in mind for the solstice this year was the setting of our new sundial. This was a Christmas gift that came without instructions; in late winter I had slogged out through two feet of snow and screwed it to a post in the garden, pointed the *N* on its engraved surface approximately north, and left it that way, figuring I'd formalize things when frostbite was less imminent. After the snow went, I realigned it with a pocket compass, and thereafter checked it occasionally: the only agreement with clock time came somewhere around noon. Whenever I noticed that it disagreed with my watch, I'd adjust it, rotating the *N* on the dial this way and that. All over the place. So I was looking forward to high noon on the solstice, at which time I would solemnly set the dial by time as well as direction, and leave it that way. Not that I expected chronometric accuracy from a sundial—I just wanted to bring it up to the standards of a stopped clock, i.e., correct once a day. *Half* a stopped clock, now that I think of it: with a twelve-hour dial, a stopped clock is right twice a day, isn't it? I don't have a good head for this stuff.

For that reason, I figured I'd better do a little research before the fact. As a first step, I looked up the correction for magnetic north on a geodetic survey map of the area. No wonder the pocket compass led me wrong: in these precincts, magnetic north is cocked fifteen degrees to the west—or it was in 1972, the date of my map; no telling where it had wandered off to by now. Even more confusing was the fact that geographic north was a degree and a half east of the pole star, if I read the map symbols correctly. I wondered if this was true elsewhere, or a phenomenon of New England. Maybe, it occurred to me, Polaris moves around too: precession and all that.

So I looked up precession—a term I dimly remembered from fifth grade science. Something about the wobble of a spinning top. *Precession,* says Webster's, is "a comparatively slow gyration of the rotation axis of a spinning body about another line intersecting it so as to describe a cone caused by the application of torque tending to change the direction of the rotation axis." Well. I sat and stared at that sentence for a while. Okay, forget about north, what we're interested in here is time, not direction. Right?

I browsed on, turning to Funk & Wagnalls. Solstice (*sol,* sun + *status,* to stop, stand still) is defined as one of two points in the ecliptic at which the sun is the greatest distance from the celestial equator. I had that image clear enough in my mind, the spinning earth tilting slowly forward, increasing the length of the day and decreasing the length of the night. Gradually presenting our face more and more to the sun—until one day it creaks to a halt, then heads back the other way. I've actually tried to imagine I could feel the judder, the change of direction: the earth as carnival ride. Funk & Wagnalls' Index sent me onward, chasing words. The little spike that casts the shadow on the sundial is the *gnomon,* from the Greek for interpreter, or pointer. The *ecliptic* is the apparent great circle annual path of the sun in the celestial sphere, as seen from the earth. The ecliptic intersects the celestial equator at two points, known as *nodes,* or *equinoxes.* Now we're getting somewhere. The plane of the ecliptic—the plane the moon must be on, or near, for eclipses to occur—intersects the celestial equator at an angle of twenty-three degrees twenty-seven minutes, which angle is known, magnificently, as the *obliquity of the ecliptic.* And so on. The obliquity of the ecliptic, I discover, is decreasing at the rate of forty-eight seconds of arc every hundred years, and will continue to do so until it reaches twenty-two degrees fifty-four minutes, after which it will start increasing again. Hold still, damn it. (One thinks of Galileo, muttering under his breath.) I am taken with a momentary fantasy about getting a sextant and learning to use it so I can take daily fixes to be sure our house has not drifted out of place overnight. As well as I can count it out on the geodetic survey map, we're at about latitude forty-two degrees thirty minutes eighteen seconds north, and longitude seventy-two degrees forty-six minutes fifty-four seconds west. Or however you write those numbers. Maybe just writing them down will conjure the house permanently in place. If I could break the map's code, I could probably figure out where my house is to the meter, but that's more accuracy than seems called for. No harm in its formal address drifting around a few hundred meters this way or that, so long as it doesn't move off this hill. Back in college the legend had it that after heavy drinking, you should lie down with one hand on the floor beside the bed, to prevent its spinning, and then shine your desk lamp at the ceiling and look at that, to hold it steady too; that way you could fall asleep without having to throw up— nausea being the result of disconnection from one's ordinary alignments.

My father, Ralph Jerome, navigated Oklahoma oil fields by dead reckoning (an elision from *deduced reckoning*), but most of the Southwest is a cinch that way, laid out in section lines, one mile square, smack on the compass lines. (The properties he traded were thus described precisely: NE/4 NE/4 SW/4 Section 17-5N-4W, McClain County. I inherited .01333 etc. mineral acres of royalty interest in that particular location. If a well is ever drilled there, it will be given a name, such as

the Ruby Jones—becoming, as soon as a hole is bored into
its depths, a real place instead of a string of numbers.) Friends
of ours invited a Kansan to their cottage an hour or so north
of New York City. The Kansan arose early, by habit. Nobody
else was up, so he went for a walk. When he returned, they
asked where he'd gone. "Well," he said, "I walked south for
about a mile, then headed east for fifteen minutes, and came
back the same way." My friends were horrified; the cottage
had been in the family for generations, but none of them had
any idea where their Kansas visitor had been, not even which
way he left the house when he started out.

I worked briefly as a technical writer in the missile business.
We were told of the wonders of inertial guidance—gyroscopes
nested within gyroscopes, quartz windows (to reduce distortion)
that allowed star sightings from the bowels of missile silos—
but not how anything actually worked. We were also told,
anecdotally, of a tracking system proposed for Florida. At right
angles from the launch point, radio beacons would be installed
at exactly one thousand meters, ten thousand meters, and one
hundred thousand meters. Signals to these points (or maybe it
was from them—I wasn't too hot as a tech writer) would indicate
precisely where our rockets were headed. The system didn't
work, and had to be abandoned: Florida is built on shifting
sands, and the radio beacons moved around too much.

The fledgling science of biomechanics attempts to apply
physics to physiology. One of its major problems is the difficulty
of precise measurement. Flesh is much too squishy. Or maybe
locating things within the flesh is a poetic rather than a scientific enterprise. When I was regularly wracking my body
athletically, I took it in to get it rolfed, which is a kind of deep
tissue massage more formally known as "structural reintegra-

tion," or realignment. It aims at reorganizing the body more carefully around the center of gravity. Because its processes and results can't quite be measured, it is often dismissed as mystical. It was a wonderful experience, and I loved it. Yoga, and the positions for sitting meditation in Zen and other Buddhisms, place great emphasis on alignment of the spine. Keeping the spine straight is regarded as a necessity in the search for enlightenment. You must let the energies flow, and they flow best in a straight line. I'm not too sure what I think about any of that—but paying *attention* to your alignment, or otherwise getting your mind fixed on some process in the present tense, now that's another matter.

In my college days I remember being romantically swept away by the image of a "still centre"—from Stephen Spender's volume of poetry with that title. I tried to envision my innermost point, if not the psychic then at least the physiological center of my body. Recently I've enjoyed reading about polar exploration, in which great squabbles arose over whether this person or that one had actually reached this or that snow-covered point—snow-covered number, really, a set of coordinates in a featureless landscape. On a map I have of Antarctica, geographers—or perhaps it was poets—have indicated a "Pole of Inaccessibility," a kind of geographic still center, I suppose, in those frozen wastes. It's in the middle of absolute nowhere, of course, around latitude eighty-two degrees south, longitude fifty-seven degrees east: the place that someone decided was farthest from . . . what? Us?

My map puts its altitude at 3,719 meters. Mt. Uttermost, let's call it, whether there's a mountain there or not. At 3,719 meters—over twelve thousand feet—it's a mountain, whether that mountain is exposed or buried in ice, whether that mountain is nothing *but* ice. A mountain peak being a point in space (and every bit as arbitrary as a pole). We've been arguing about how tall Mt. Everest is ever since we've known there was a Mt. Everest. In the latest round we used lasers and satellites to do the measuring, and added a few feet. But then Mt. Everest is still growing. It's probably moving around, too.

Along about this point in my research, the sound of the town's noon whistle came drifting up the valley. I grabbed my pocket compass and trotted out to the garden—wasting a good fifteen seconds, but there's no sweep second hand on a sundial. I wrenched the dial around so the shadow of the gnomon pointed exactly at the numeral *12*, and tightened down the mounting screw: there, nailed in place, locked down and permanent. The whole procedure gave me this wonderful feeling that I'd drawn a line straight down through the center of the year.

At 1:00 P.M. I checked the time again, and at one-thirty, and two; still reasonably accurate. By three-thirty it was getting a little slow, and by four-thirty was almost twenty minutes off. Oh well. I figured the error would be the same during the morning hours, but in the other direction. Wouldn't it? Days *are* symmetrical, aren't they?

Later I found out that a sundial has to be designed for its specific location, and even then requires tables to convert solar time to local standard time. It's a more primitive instrument than I had realized, surviving not out of any utility but only as a symbol of the ambitions of our forebears in the direction of science. Trying to make one accurate is a little like trying to levitate one of our sugar maples: basically silly. But then so is wall-building, when it's not to keep the goddamned cows in. That's okay. My sundial was accurate enough. I checked it every time I passed by, all summer long, taking great pleasure at being so accurately aligned with the globe and the solar system. It wasn't until late October that I realized that the clock I used to set it by had been on daylight saving time.

[7]

J U L Y :

S W I N G S

House guests arrived for the Fourth of July. The father confessed that on the drive up, he had suggested the possibility of a swing to five-year-old Sarah. Amuse-a-Child Projects, Inc.: tie a couple of ropes on a maple limb, hang a board seat between. Sounded like a good idea to me. Unlike stone work, this was a project for which I had experience.

The best available maple limb—level, with a clear space below—was twelve feet off the ground, and there wasn't enough decent rope around the place to do the job. We zipped in to the hardware store for some real rope, stout half-inch hemp (an old-fashioned item now, among the spools of gangrenous-looking plastics). Got home, fetched ladders, tied each end carefully in place, notched a piece of two-by-six to slip into the loop to make a level seat. Deposited Sarah on it, gave her a push: a fine-looking swing, but it didn't want to go straight. No matter how carefully you pushed, it quickly picked up a wobble, attempted to rotate, began yanking its small passenger around in an unsettling fashion. This was unsatisfactory. A swing should be smooth.

It would do fine for twirling—when you lie on your belly across the seat of the swing and twist up the ropes like the rubberband of a model airplane, until the seat is raised so high your toes will no longer get a sufficient grip on the ground, and then you pick up your feet and let go, unwinding. (Remember how the last rotation comes with a jerk, as the twisted ropes spring apart and drop the seat the last few inches? And how if you catch that last rotation just right, you can dig in a toe and give the swing a kick that starts it winding up again in the opposite direction? And how after twenty or thirty cycles of this, how far away your imagination would go, as you lay there across the seat of the swing, fighting nausea?) Our new swing was fine for that, but not for swinging.

We broke for lunch—minus Sarah, who continued field research on twirling—and considered the mechanics of swings. What was the flaw that was throwing the swing off line? After a sandwich I strolled back out, beer in hand, observing. The limb was eight inches in diameter. The righthand rope gripped the limb tightly, so the axis of its swing was at the bottom of the limb's thickness; the lefthand rope, more loosely tied, was slipping back and forth with each swing, pivoting at the top of the limb, eight inches higher. The limb was not, after all, the level axle that is required for straight swinging. Tightening the lefthand rope stopped it from slipping, which straightened the swing right out. Perfected. To finish up the job, I wrapped the loose ends of the rope with friction tape to prevent unraveling, because that's the way my father always did it.

There remained only to teach Sarah to pump—to swing herself—after which we wouldn't see much of her for the rest of the visit. To pump a swing you lean back, pulling with your arms, then forward, then back again, and first thing you know you're swinging. The arc is tiny at first, but grows. The trick is to catch this small motion and enhance it, picking up a little more altitude on each cycle, swooping higher and higher. Easy. Much easier than explaining it to a five-year-old. Solution: take the five-year-old on your lap, and do it. Dad did, and she picked up the rhythm quickly enough.

My son, Marty, also came out for the weekend, from his magazine job in the city, arriving that night, missing out on the engineering of the swing. I had larger projects in mind for him anyway. There was still a few feet of gap in the stone wall, and I'd vowed—aloud, with witnesses—I'd get it finished by the Fourth of July. Marty is large and strong enough, a healthy young man, and I thought he might find a taste of stone work interesting. You know, wrestle stones for a while, bust a sweat, then go for a swim and a beer, that kind of summery thing. (Male bonding, I can hear Chris mutter to herself, eyes cutting skyward.) So I announced casually at breakfast that I was going to get in another couple of loads of stone, and anyone who wanted could come along. Okay, said Marty, a little grunt work would do him good. Some holiday: dragooned before he'd even finished his grapefruit.

It was a gloriously hot, still morning, the midsummer sun cooking the hillside even under the maple canopy. Cicadas loud enough to make you dizzy. I tried to hold back on the pace, slow things down, in deference to the heat if not to the task; Marty kept working faster, seeing this project—not his own—as something to be completed. I tried to disabuse him of this concept, but did not succeed. Hormones, I thought. We both worked with one eye fixed on the pond, and made complicated jokes about how one judged the perfect moment, the perfect level of sweatiness at which to bolt for its cold water.

We'd brought the first load back to the wall and were fitting the stones before I noticed the ghosts working alongside us. During most of my adolescence, my stepfather held distant construction jobs, coming home only on weekends. At Saturday breakfast he would announce the day's domestic chores to my mother, speaking of me, and describing my participation in the tasks, in the third person. We lived then on a small rural acreage that required constant heavy maintenance: mowing, cutting brush, pruning, fencing, and other construction for our slapdash menagerie of chickens, dogs, a couple of pigs. I hated it, hated every moment of the work Ott and I did together. My grudging participation couldn't have been that helpful, particularly in my early teens. I think he was just trying to build my character. Now, forty years later, I was thunderstruck to find myself replicating the pattern, unthinkingly, with my own adult son. The difference was that once I recognized it, we joked about it as we worked. My stepfather and I had never joked.

"How do you, um, put them on here?" Marty asked, as we were filling the gap in the wall. On what theory does one fit stones? I couldn't say. One on two, two on one, I said, just fill the space, don't worry about it. We tossed stones at a more or less furious rate, Marty's eagerness infecting me, too. A second load, and in a total of about an hour we had filled out the missing piece, giving a nice sense of completeness to the line between the poplars and the trellis. The next segment of wall would pick up on the other side of the trellis. I'd start it next week.

We weren't yet completely bushed, and I suggested one other little piece of stone work. When Chris and I bought the place, there were two large granite stones lying beside the head of the driveway, each about six feet long and more than a foot square in cross-section. I had mowed around them for several years before I realized they were old gate posts that had fallen over. At a hundred and fifty pounds per cubic foot, these stones had to weigh at least eight or nine hundred pounds apiece, and until I started doing stone work I had considered them much too large to be moved. I still didn't want to move them very far, but it occurred to me that they'd look better standing up than lying down, and would simplify the mowing in the bargain. Besides, figuring out how to erect them would be interesting.

We started with the one on the right side of the driveway, and it went very smoothly. It was half buried in the ground; we pried it out and slipped rollers under it, dug a foundation hole, rolled it up to the edge of the hole, and began tilting it. For the first few degrees of arc, we used crowbars and two-by-fours to pry it, then switched to muscle as it approached its balance point on the lip. The only time we had to exert much real force was in raising the upper end the last foot or so before the stone tipped over into the hole. It slipped right in, and we tamped it solidly in place. Dead easy. Scylla, I began calling it: a piece of cake, taking us maybe thirty minutes. We were sweaty now, and it was time for a swim. I'd do Charybdis later, in a day or two, I said.

My father was a connoisseur of swings. Memory surely exaggerates, but I seem to recall that he would cheerfully drive me across a good piece of Oklahoma just to give me the experience of a particularly fine rope swing. He was especially interested in the ones located over water—ideally, on a riverbank bluff above a pretty swimming hole. I think he collected swings the way people collect suspension bridges or hexagonal barns. He traveled the state endlessly anyway, an oil-lease broker dickering with farmers over minuscule shares of mineral rights. Pick a road going out of Oklahoma City in any direction, and he seemed to be able to come up with a rope swing about every twenty or thirty miles along the route.

It never occurred to me to wonder whether he actually sampled these discoveries out of my company. When I was four, my mother left him and moved my ten-year-old brother Jud and me to Houston. Thereafter Jud and I saw him only in summertime. Swings and swimming holes were the lure, the entertainment to guarantee the success of our summer visits. He and Evelyn, my new stepmother, once provided adult supervision for Jud's Boy Scout patrol on a two-week camping trip to southeastern Oklahoma—six or seven early adolescents and tagalong me, by then about eight years old. We erected one elaborate campsite, then razed it and lugged everything a couple of miles downstream on the Mountain Fork River, just so we could re-establish ourselves on an appropriate twelve-foot bluff, with a tree arching out nicely over the deep part of the river. We put up a world-class rope swing that time—my father as engineer—and pretty well ignored the woods and wildlife around us for the rest of the trip.

The next swing that I can remember was over-engineered. Ralph and Evelyn had moved to a small cottage outside of Oklahoma City, on a terraced hillside with a really huge oak tree for shade. He wrote me about it. Jud would be off in college that summer, and he'd have to be at the office a lot, but if I wanted to come up, I might enjoy the *trapeze*! He described it in detail. He'd spotted this perfect limb, nearly thirty feet up. He'd bought brand new rope, scrambled all the way up that scary height, and hung not one but two ropes.

He'd spliced metal rings to the bottom ends, and then somewhere found a genuine whiffletree, from the harness for a draft horse, to snap into the metal rings as the crossbar of a trapeze. I'd better come give this contraption a try, he said. It wasn't over water—no soaring flight at the end—but as pure swing, it was the cat's pajamas.

In practice, the physics weren't right. Maybe it was just the air resistance of those long, long ropes. (I was a skinny twelve by then, and didn't add a great deal of mass to the mechanism.) Pumping with great effort, I'd get it going fairly high, but the moment I stopped working, it would drag to a stop. With that long reach to the ropes, I felt more like a kite than the weight on a pendulum anyway.

That summer's trapeze went through several permutations before we decided that the second rope was confusing the issue, making things too complicated. The classic great swings in history, after all, were single ropes; just look at any Tarzan movie. We took down one rope, and tied a gunnysack full of rags to the bottom of the other one, giving a soft seat you could straddle with your legs. Then we had a terrific swing, but only if you had someone to help you swing—since you can't pump a single-rope swing, and we lacked the requisite river bluff. At home alone, I finally learned to tie the spare rope onto the bottom of the swing, climb with the end of the rope as high as I dared onto a suitable other limb, haul the swing up, and let fly. A great swing, but only I would use it: my father, who had climbed to hang the swing in the first place, for some reason wouldn't venture out on shaky limbs to give it a try. Frankly, I was a little disappointed in him.

———

There are two docks in our pond, fifty meters apart; Marty and I cruise back and forth in the swimming equivalent of a loafing jog, alternating laps, passing in the middle, careful not to imply anything like a race. The top eighteen inches of the pond is bearably warm, but bubbles of cold spring water rise to the surface here and there, and when you hit one there is a natural tendency to put on a bit of a sprint to the next warm spot. After a few circuits I have had enough, and fetch a couple of beers from the house. I sit on the end of one of the docks, watching dragonflies dart and hover. Red-winged blackbirds, flushed out of the nearby cattails, heap curses on our heads. High summer. Marty stops for a swallow of beer, then flips over and sets out on another lap. I feel a flush of gratitude and pleasure, watching his graceful stroke curve across the water. Wondering how, without my hovering presence, he learned to swim so well.

He was seven when his mother and I were divorced; I eventually remarried and moved out of the city, and he became, with sisters Kate and Julie, a regular summer visitor. During the summer visits of my children, work was banished: we ran and played, jumped in swimming holes. No chores. (Stepmother Chris excepted, of course; in those days it never occurred to me that meals wouldn't just appear on schedule.) If the kids were to learn about work, it would be from their single-parent mother back home, teaching school, often as not working two jobs; when it came to character-building, I had skipped town. From their mother they learned, I think, that you work for what you get, what you have. If they learned anything from me, maybe it was that you work at what you can't resist working on. I hope so; that's what I kept telling them anyway, when I had the chance. I have no idea what they actually did learn from me, about anything. I doubt any parent really does. As young adults, they work hard now, have always worked hard, on the model of their mother. None of them has quite been seized, I think, by the work so far available to them. I wish I had taught them . . . better? Something else?

___

In addition to rope swings, my father pursued the perfect ice cream. After supper we would sometimes drive in to downtown Oklahoma City to visit some drugstore where he'd heard they did a particularly good job with, say, fresh peach. (The only time I ever heard the word "larruping" spoken aloud was from his mouth—around, and in praise of, an especially satisfactory spoonful of ice cream.) He was also a drunk, whose excesses regularly and consistently splintered other people's lives, but he would stop to do things—swing on rope swings, eat ice cream, sing old songs on the back stoop on summer evenings— for the direct sensory enjoyment. He was a passionate fly fisherman, practicing his casts endlessly in the backyard for the simple sensuous pleasure of working the curl of the line. I can't recall ever seeing my stepfather, a steadfast working man, do anything for pleasure.

The real reason my father drove me all over Oklahoma on hot summer days was not to demonstrate swings but to talk to people, to make deals. I never caught on to how unhappy his life was. I loved him because he was my father, and forgave him his frequent drunken violations of my happiness. I never realized that his work consisted of empty transactions, cleverness, sweating to get an edge on people. My stepfather, Ott, worked terribly hard all the time, twelve- and fourteen-hour days, and then came home and sat at his drafting board, designing more things to build. (I showed no interest in the drawings; he never showed them to me.) He probably had a satisfactory and interesting life, but I never was aware of him enjoying a day of it. My father came home—often, already drunk—and listened to the radio and read *Reader's Digest*.

My father taught me—if not explicitly then by example, in his celebration of occasional small successes—that work was mostly a matter of being smarter than other people. Not more intelligent, not wiser, but in the sense of quickness, as in smart as a whip. Another common expression of his era was "crooked as a dog's hind leg." Crookedness was simultaneously despised and admired. I don't know if he was crooked. (My mother came finally to think he was.) His favorite book was *The Gentle Grafter*. Not long before I was born, Pretty Boy Floyd still roamed the Oklahoma hills, enjoying a certain folk-hero status.

My father and I worked hard at building those swings. It was the only physical work I ever recall seeing him do. My stepfather taught me that work was what you did to hold back the tide, to keep from being swept under. He was—to me, anyway—unlovable and cold, and I never caught on to the fact that he was working for pleasure. Never saw that he was getting what he needed from that, in his stolid, silent way, and didn't need us, or social contact, or much else. (In fact he was conspicuously ill at ease in social situations.) Both men, it amuses me now to think, lived in hot climates: Ralph had a hammock under a shade tree, and used it now and then; I doubt Ott could have conceived of owning a hammock. (I have a hammock and never use it.) Of the two men, Ott was the stabler, productive one, who never hurt anybody—although he never comforted anyone much either—but whom I could not understand. So I loved my father and hated my stepfather. Both of them died before I had a chance to think about them enough.

After close observation of, and grudging participation in, my stepfather's concept of useful work, I decided that it, likewise, was a hateful thing—buying into that folklore the way some people buy into fundamentalist religion—and I determined to be a mental rather than a physical person. It was a more agreeable method of managing the world than all that grunting, sweaty stuff, I thought. It sent me to college, and the city.

For some reason the mental life didn't pan out. I could make a living from it, in the sense of avoiding manual labor as a principal means of support, but its pleasures and satisfactions failed to measure up to those available from more concretely grounded pursuits. Perhaps I am wired wrong, the major satisfactions coming through the nerve endings of the musculoskeletal system, rather than through the nerve endings inside the cranium where all that tedious thinking goes on. The world, after all, is full of things that I feel I should be able to understand but can't; the world is not so full of things that I feel I should be able to move but can't.

This is a disappointment. Somewhere—probably in contrarian response to my stepfather—I got the idea that what mental effort was supposed to provide was some kind of truth, some kind of solid, dependable information I could bank on. But the more I pursued mental activities, the less reliable the information became. The more I strived to develop the objectivity and fair-mindedness that were supposed to allow me to see things clearly, the less resolution I seemed to be able to lay my hands on. Physical effort, on the other hand, seemed more and more to be making available a kind of direct, solid, reliable truth—if only trueness in the carpenter's sense.

Objectively, my father was the awful man of the two, but from where I sat, this was completely reversed. If I tell half of Ralph's story I make him a dear man; if I tell the other half I make him a monster. Only the monster part applied through most of my formative years, but I choose to remember the other. I can't make Ott a dear man; I never made any contact with that part of him. When I try to see that part, looking through other people's eyes, I suffer a complete failure of compassion. Ott probably shaped me more than Ralph did, having more years in which to accomplish it. Now, needing to make a small repair to the tractor, I trudge back to the house for tools, and feel Ott's body in my walk, and immediately change my gait, trying to exorcise him. I hear Ralph's voice in my own and try to weed it out, shudder when I see my brother's knobby, aging hands on the ends of my wrists. Please, let me be unique. I left the Southwest as one runs away from home, worked hard to remove the southernness from my speech. I have been a schmoozer, as my deal-making father was, as is required of a journalist. I have also tried to disappear in solitary physical work, as in building walls. Neither strategy is very satisfactory. If I am so determined to be unique, why am I still trying to be both those men at once?

In my own (limited) parenting days, I bought a swing set or two, those flimsy, tin-can, discount-store affairs. (Julie, my youngest, knocked out two front teeth on one. They were horribly dangerous and, I assume, are banned by now.) I don't think that kind of swing set was generally available in the Depression, but we preferred the larger playground models anyway, made out of stout pipe and chain. A decent playground swing was big enough for two kids, standing up, facing each other, pumping so high the swing would stall out, losing the centrifugal force that kept the chains taut. When it did, it would start falling back through the arc: a sickening little float at the top and then a lurching snap as we hit the ends of the chains again. The idea was to go so high you scared each other, daring each other to go higher yet. This recreation was particularly effective with girl partners. We also climbed the poles, both for the novel view of the playground and for the pleasant sensations that developed in the groin during the process of shinnying up the poles, forecasting amazing pleasures to come. (Or at least the boys did this. I never had the courage to ask girls if they'd noticed anything like that. But then I don't recall girls shinnying up the swing poles.) And we jumped out of playground swings, without benefit of water to land in, for the less subtle but more readily available thrill of flight, slipping out of the seat at progressively greater altitudes, exploring the borderline where the pain of landing began to conflict with the pleasure of flying. On playground swings, the occasions of sin lay all about us, inviting the usual experimental science.

Rope swings were better, though. I have examined our pond carefully for a tree limb that will support one, but none exists. There are only curving birches—conjuring up Robert Frost— that terminate tantalizingly short of the water. Jud, who went on to become a poet, once decided to explicate Frost at a Caribbean cocktail party by becoming a swinger of palm-trees. Palms being less flexible than birches, one finally broke, and he came crashing to the pool deck, breaking a foot. Paradoxically, he had broken the other foot years before when some adults, moving the frame of a swing set, dropped one of the heavy pipes on it. Jud has reasons not to like swings anymore, I suppose.*

I guess I still do; at any rate I haven't yet escaped the pattern. After my divorce I found myself searching out swings and swimming holes for the use of my visiting kids. It became something of a family joke. The best swimming hole we ever

---

*This just in: Jud says he wasn't explicating Frost, he was arguing about the Trinity, and needed a higher pulpit. And besides, it wasn't a palm, it was a papaya.

found was spotted at sixty miles an hour out the back window
of our speeding car. Someone saw a glimmer of blue-green
winking through the woods; I made a screeching U-turn, and
we then spent a glorious summer afternoon in the Saco, ex-
perimenting with the physics of river flow—no swing, in this
case, being available.

In my high-school days I lived for, and in, a river called
the Comal, in New Braunfels, Texas, which was full of superb
swimming holes. My mother, Gwen, lived out her life in New
Braunfels, and long after I had left, Kate, Marty, and Julie,
for whom this was all relatively foreign territory, met me there
for her funeral. It was late spring, and hot and beautiful, and
we found an occasion to slip away from the formalities for a
swim. The river had changed a great deal in the thirty-five
years since I'd known it daily, but the water was still clear
and cold. I did it just for the swim, I thought at the time, but
with the unacknowledged hope that my kids would understand
that Gwen had loved to swim in that river as much as I, and
make some kind of connection out of that. The swimming hole
we chose happened to have a moderately good rope swing, and
we all took a couple of turns. It wasn't until I woke with aching
muscles the next day, from the unaccustomed pull of the swing,
that I began making the connections for myself. All those years,
that woman, those two men.

[8]

AUGUST:

RIGGING

There are some things to know about this business after all, besides the stuff about two on one, one on two. When laying up new wall, use your heavier stones first, down low, lifting them no higher than necessary. Save flat stones for the top, stones with vertical sides or square corners for the ends. Use misshapen, irregular stones for footings, turning their flattest sides up. Leave an inch or two of space between footing stones for drainage, but chink the spaces with rubble. When possible, lay stones so the upper surface is slanted toward the center line of the wall; then gravity will pull the wall together rather than apart. Every six feet or so, lay a long stone across the width of the wall as a tie-stone, to help hold the whole thing together. If a stone wobbles, you can shim it with smaller rocks, but it'll be more stable if you chip away the bump that causes the wobble instead. Total control. (Stonemason John Vivian calls these bumps "wobble knobs." Sounds like something out of a children's book, says Chris: Thumbknuckle and the Wobble-Knobs.) Don't work when the stones are wet, or the ground slippery. (Exception: if you're using a gangplank to load stones, they'll slide easier if you wet the plank.) Wear gloves and steel-toed shoes. When you get tired, stop.

"For a period of a little more than a year I constructed dry-stone walls on a large upland farm in northwest Yorkshire," says Andrew Shaughnessy:

> During that time I lived in a simple stone cottage. I stepped back in time then; walking across the dewy morning fields, I fancied that I recaptured something of the atmosphere of 200 years gone. I became sun-browned in the summer and chilled to the very marrow on many a sharp winter day. There were long periods given over to quiet reflection, remote as I was from the sounds of the busy world.
>
> In certain ways it was an idyllic time for me and served to teach me an important lesson. I learned that life need not be rushed at as though tomorrow would never come. Wall-building is not something that lends itself to hurry and speed; it requires a steady, methodical approach which if not adhered to will result in aching backs and squashed fingers. I learned the virtue of patience that year in my work on the old dry-stone walls. (From "A Yorkshire Legacy" *Country Journal*, May, 1986.)

That's what I want, the way I wish I lived. What is it that keeps it from being like that for me? What is it in me that keeps it from being like that?

———

In search of a long, unpressured, summer Saturday, I get an early start, waiting only for the dew to dry before hitching up the wagon. I toss in pinch bars, planks, and rollers, and head up the lane, passing work sites where the old wall has been gapped, by my previous raids. As the tractor grinds past these gaps, I nod in acknowledgment: I have spent some interesting time there, wrestling stones. I came to know the contours of that immediate ground very well. Each gap marks the edge of a twenty-foot circle within which I know every bump and hollow, the location of individual roots that tried to trip me up. It is real estate that I have come to own a little differently than I do the property described in the courthouse deed.

The next work site is just past the first steep uphill stretch of road. I tried, earlier, taking stones from the steep pitch. That was a mistake. It was ten times harder to get the wagon backed in and the tractor securely chocked in place, to get my feet under me to move stones, to keep stones from getting away. When the ground is steep, you work on a sidehill, no matter which way the slope goes. Sidehills are tough. (Ask a golfer or a skier.) They complicate immeasurably those physical tasks that are difficult enough without gravity pulling at you from the wrong angle. Not only was working on the steep slope awkward, but the problems it presented were not particularly worth solving, with plenty of other fine stones to be had only a little farther up the lane. But it did tug at my cheapskate's soul to abandon good stones only because they were too much trouble. Up in the woods at the top of the loop, there's a fine piece of abandoned wall that runs straight down the fall line of a very steep slope. When I look at it, when I think of the work of putting it there, it almost makes me want to cry.

———

"We used to have 'stone bees,' when all the men of a village or hamlet came together with their draft cattle, and united to clear some patch of earth which had been stigmatized by nature

with an undue visitation of stones and rocks," wrote one Samuel
Griswold Goodrich in 1856. "All this labor was gratuitously
rendered, save only that the proprietor of the land furnished
the grog. Such a meeting was always of course a very social
and sociable affair. When the work was done, gymnastic ex-
ercises—such as hopping, wrestling, and foot-racing—took
place among the athletic young men."

After the steep spot there's a stretch of nearly level ground. I
get the wagon into place, set up a gangplank, haul out tools,
look around for an appropriate stone to start off with. And then
stop and remind myself that the point isn't just to work in a
cool niche in the woods, nice as that is to do, but also to try
to listen, smell, watch. I pause, formally, to inspect a small
spider web hanging in front of my face, the web proper about
five inches in diameter, the tiny spider barely visible in it.
The web itself, though, is tied in place to trees and stones
across a fifteen-foot gap, an extravagant expenditure of rigging
for such a tiny place of business. Whatever happened to nature's tight energy budgets?

Not in August, I guess. It's about as glorious as it ever gets
in the woods, hot and still in the sun but cool enough in the
shade that work at a moderate pace stays comfortable. Inviting,
perhaps, grandiose web placements. I load up with small
stones, which have a certain cocktail-peanut effect, tempting
me to load the wagon too heavily. I haul them down and dump
them by the new wall and go back to the woods for another
load, this time of larger, more interesting stones. These I spread
out alongside the wall so I can see what I've got. And begin
staring at them, trying to see where they'll go.

With a good selection of large stones spread across the
grass—and, this morning, anyway, the right frame of mind—

fitting them into the wall becomes a geometric game. Rocks this size are not conveniently liftable, so I move them mostly by flipping them: turning them up on edge and letting them flop, side over side or end over end. Their irregular shapes make them easier to flip in some directions than others, which means I move them not in a straight line but a meandering path. When I have picked out a rock and a place to move it to, I then try to envision how to get it there with the lowest number of flips—preferably while having to flip as few other stones as possible out of the way. But I don't stop and think any of this out, it's just the constant free-form play going on in the mind as I mess around with the rocks. It's a slow, gentle, multidimensional chess match with the natural world, working easily in the hot sun, even relishing the heat. No straining allowed. Sometimes it goes exactly right.

———

And sometimes it doesn't. Almost anywhere around the place I go, I pass the site of some semi-crazed work burst in the past. Most of these involved a chainsaw at some point. The worst is a hundred-foot cut in the line of trees between two fields. A couple of years ago I decided to clear out a small patch of grapevine-entangled trash trees, to open a sight-line between the fields. I optimistically estimated the job would take half a day. In four hours I had cut perhaps a tenth of what would be required, and was already working in a kind of growing physical hysteria, fatigued into stupidity.

I'd sawed through half a dozen five-inch saplings that had snagged at a forty-five-degree angle, their crowns so entangled they couldn't fall. I figured that monkeying up the top side of one of the slanted trunks would surely bring them all sliding the rest of the way down. I shinnied up—six feet, ten feet, fifteen feet. Didn't work. I tried bouncing, working the leaning tree like a diving board, to gain more force. That didn't work either. I began working my way from slanting trunk to slanting trunk, trying to find at least one that would come loose, still hoping it might drag the others with it. When I finally fell out of the bundle of tangled trees, one of my wrists caught in a forked branch, leaving me unhurt but hanging by one arm, my boots a couple of feet off the ground, sweat pouring into my eyes, blackflies beginning to feast on my exposed rib cage as I tried to figure out how to get myself down. Later I would hire a couple of local farm youths to finish the job for the cordwood and twenty dollars. It may have been the best twenty bucks I ever spent.

That is, there may be an impression of competence gathering about this narrative, and I wouldn't want anyone to be misled. Physical projects don't always work out smoothly around here. I am never confident of their outcome. I had to raise the corner of the garage recently—never mind why—and came up with a perfectly sensible if somewhat jury-rigged solution involving a couple of stout planks wedged against the juncture of walls and rafters, and a hydraulic jack. It looked safe enough to me, any way I could figure it, but as I began cranking away at the jack—taking up all that weight and beginning to apply real force, the building creaking as it began to rise—I shuddered involuntarily, and found myself thinking, *shouldn't the big boys be doing this?*

The hydraulic jack, as a device for lifting frighteningly heavy objects, invariably leads to such speculations. Years ago I restored an old truck and used the jack a great deal for that. In one (customary) flurry of hyper-efficiency, I started letting the truck down off the jack while I was still in the act of sliding out from under it. I was lying on my side on a creeper; the descending front bumper caught my upper shoulder and began to fold me in two, trying to close me like a book. I was almost clear, though, and managed to wrench free—spit out across the garage floor like a watermelon seed—just before real pain set in. Afterward, I remember sitting on the creeper against the far garage wall, staring at the truck and the jack, thinking very hard. (A few days later I would hop lightly down from a perch on the truck's fender and break my foot, but no jack was involved in that particular misadventure.)

———

There's a stone at the top of the loop—not far from the steep pitch—that I want and can't quite get. It'd make a fine threshold or capstone: nice and flat, three feet by four feet, maybe six inches thick. It is too far back in the woods and too large in the bargain, and it is driving me crazy. Every time I see it I start designing a roadway, trying to figure out how to get my wagon to it, how to get it into the wagon. The sight of it always starts me inventing rigging.

This is a wonderfully addictive mental activity. I am not an insomniac—I normally go to sleep like a bowling ball rolling off a table—but I've learned never to start planning mechanical projects when I lie down at night. It is too seductive. My brain gets inflamed with inventing angles and joints in the night, calculating where this will brace against that and how I will bolt it together, and before long only my heels and the back of my head are touching the sheets, and my nightclothes are all sweaty.

Not that the projects that keep me awake are likely to get carried out. I'm not good at rigging. Sound carpentry (equal parts rigging and joinery) continues to elude me. I always end up using lumber that is too large or too small for the job, into which I put the wrong size nails, so the wood splits. I can do the work okay—drive the nails, saw out the marks—but I always forget some critical angle of bracing, or misestimate loadings. I haven't got the engineering for it. What I really lack, though (and have trouble admitting it), is not information or training so much as a certain ready grasp of the way things work. It is an instinct, deeper than rules, I think. When I'm tying the canoe to the top of the car—a quintessential problem in rigging—I am haunted by the certainty that there are better knots than the ones I've used, and better places to tie the ropes. When someone improves one of my lash-ups, as often happens, I feel like a jerk not to have seen the obvious solution myself.

We had some remodeling done. Richard, the contractor, worked more in his head and less with pencil and paper than I expected in so large a project. We'd be discussing some feature in the new kitchen, and I'd ask him if he could do this or that. His eyes would glaze slightly as he called up the hidden structure, and the modification of it, in his mind. Sometimes he would make small gestures with his hands, without saying a word, as he thought of how this joint or that would go, what would brace which. It was wonderful to watch. Often he would stand still for minutes before he told me whether he could do what we wanted, or what would be the best way to accomplish our request. He was in the unfortunate position of having to be on the job every day. His co-workers were perfectly competent, but he was the one who had planned out the job in his head and ordered the materials for it, and there was no way, he told me, that he could write down, or tell the others ahead of time, how it was supposed to go. He had to be there for it step by step as it unfolded. Because of this quirk in his working method, we got a lot of very high-level manual labor out of Richard.

Carpentry is a much more complex pastime than stone work,

and the sizes and appropriate uses of the materials barely
scratch the surface of what I don't know about it. Still, I have
a better physical sense than some. I can change light switches,
do minor repairs, keep machines running. The rough carpentry
that I do, though (and I attempt no other kind), has a loose
and sloppy feel to it, a sense of approximation when it is done.
With professionals, it doesn't turn out that way. I admire their
work extravagantly.

When it comes to working with heavy things, I've become
judiciously afraid of trees but am still not afraid—not afraid
enough—of stones. I didn't always fear trees, little realizing
how tricky and unpredictable all that weight could be when it
starts down, how complicated and risky its management. Trees
fall slowly, majestically, their branches absorbing the force so
that they seem to be lowered to the ground, rather than smashing down. This is misleading. Makes you cocky. As a kid, as
a younger man, I thought tree-felling a simple matter. That
was before I'd gotten my saw pinched a few times and tried to
extract it, before I'd acquired much direct muscular feel for
the startling intractability of all that weight. Gravity, when you
get right down to it, is a large percentage of what work is all
about, and managing it is the first principle, the starting
place—as I relearn every time I start messing around with big
rocks. Anyway, there's still one good-sized tree sticking out
into the gap between those two fields, and I'd prefer to have
it out of there, but it is too large. It's a good fourteen inches
thick and cocks over at an odd angle, and I am afraid of it.

A great deal of this fear has to do with the chainsaw, which
pulls you along and makes you work all wrong. It's a nasty
machine. I blame it, for instance, for the time I ended up
hanging by my wrist: the chainsaw set the wrong pace from

the outset, and I was never able to regain control. There are people who come to love chainsaws, become rapturous about them and highly skilled in their use, but I am not one of them and have no plans in that regard.

Not that I mean to romanticize work done purely by hand. If it's a big job, if there's any kind of time pressure, mechanization is the only way. I accept that. But the price is always more urgency: the equipment is so expensive, so loud, sending out all these distracting signals—use me, hurry up, get this over with, get me shut off. Anyway, it probably isn't the romance of hand work but simple cheapness that makes me resist mechanization. And, in the case of the leaning tree, fear. My friend Willy says the two of us can take it down, neatly and safely, with a two-man handsaw. What's more, he says, learning to operate a two-man saw is an experience I should not miss. We'll see.

———

Richard's father ran a garage, so he grew up well grounded in that branch of mechanics; in Vietnam, he maintained and flew in carrier-based aircraft, and learned the physical systems of ships and planes. He's been building and restoring houses ever since. I think he has as sure a grasp of the real-world physical requirements of structures and machines as anyone I know. In addition to the specific skills of contracting, he fixes things. He fixed things around the house, almost in passing, that had nothing to do with the remodeling job. I got the impression that he just sees, instantly, how things work and what has gone awry.

In this I like to imagine that he is part Eskimo. (Actually, he's of French-Canadian extraction and, a canoe nut, longs as romantically for the days of the *voyageurs* as I yearn for some of Mr. Shaughnessy's patience.) Eskimos, says Barry Lopez in his book *Arctic Dreams,* are born mechanics, notorious for their quick and intuitive grasp of the physical nature of things. "Even when the object is something they've never seen before," says Lopez, "they will select from 'scrap' or 'waste' material something with the right tensile strength or capacity for torsion or elasticity, something with the necessary resistance to heat, repeated freezing or corrosion, and shape it with simple tools into a serviceable if not permanent solution. Nineteenth-century explorers remarked on this capacity often, as have modern scientists with broken outboard engines and wrist-watches.

"Very sharp, someone once said, these broadly smiling men with no pockets, no hats, and no wheels."

It is a matter, I am convinced, of getting the physics right. That's when the rigging works, when the wood doesn't split. Eskimos, by this accounting, are instinctive practical physicists. Or maybe they are better described as materials athletes. The athlete, too, is in the business of getting the physics right, of selecting, from circumstances that are rapidly changing, the right kind of force to apply for the right length of time at just the right angle and in just the right amount. Athletics concerns itself with making judgments about physical laws—acceleration and deceleration, momentum and mass, vectors of force, that kind of thing—and putting those judgments into effect. The better athlete is the one who works those laws more effectively. Nothing heroic about it. There is a silken, almost magical ease to the movements of the great athletes, instantly recognizable but not so easy to define. We credit them with almost mystical powers; they are only getting the physics right. We speak of their movements as beautiful, but what we mean is efficient. Or maybe just appropriate: the thing that rivets us, visually, in athletics—or dance, same thing—is the startling efficiency of the exactly appropriate move.

It is more pleasurable to make those moves than to watch them, of course. One gets a hint of their pleasures when a large stone slips easily into place.

I needed mechanization and didn't have it for the raising of the other gate-post stone by the driveway, which I tackled by myself. With Marty's help Scylla had been easy, but Charybdis went critical on me a long time before it reached the tipping point. In the first place, the whole process was slowed considerably because I was prying the stone up with one hand and inserting props under it with the other: not nearly as efficient as with one man prying and the other securing the gain. By myself, I had to stop to make sure the stone was in control and stable, on some kind of firm foundation, after every increment of progress. This required endless trips to fetch more blocks, planks, wedges, rollers, every solid object I could lay my hands on, to prop the stone in place.

After I'd levered one end of the stone a foot or so off the ground, the weight and the angles began to grow too severe for a (sensible) one-man operation, and I began having difficulty securing the gain. Time for the old hydraulic jack. With the smooth and gradual lifting power of hydraulics, all I had to do was put the jack under one end of the rock, crank it up through its six inches of travel, block that gain in place, let down the jack and raise *its* foundation, and crank it up some more. No problem, except that while the jack had plenty of gross lifting capacity, the business end—the top of the piston, which did the actual raising—was only an inch in diameter. The rock wanted very badly to tip and slide off one side or the other of the narrow piston, so I had to place the jack very carefully, and keep the nine-hundred-pound rock balanced with one hand while I jacked with the other. Which, most of the time, I couldn't quite manage to do. The rock kept sliding off the jack. When it did, it usually knocked most of the blocks out of the way so I had to start all over again, prying it up from ground level and blocking it in place before I could get the jack under it, and so on.

I have no idea how many times I went through this cycle, but as I gradually acquired more skill and ingenuity, I managed to get the end of the stone a little higher each time. Most of the times. Unfortunately, the higher it was when it slipped off the jack, the more force with which it fell. In the early stages the stone seemed merely to sigh and tip over on its side; after I began getting the end a couple of feet into the air, it would let go with a shuddering groan, spit the jack to the side with great force, and then crash down into the various blocks and rollers lying below, flipping them into the air, making me caper and dance out of the way. Once, too slow of foot, I didn't quite manage to dodge the flying jack, and got whacked on the shin, leaving a dark blue egg-shaped knot which, throbbing, kept trying to talk me into giving up.

I am now a physically larger and perhaps stronger man than my late stepfather ever was, with a wider experience of the world, a better education, a larger income. I nevertheless still think of him as a serious adult—one of the big boys—and myself, in relation to him, as a scrawny adolescent.

Maybe welding would help. When I was growing up, the ultimate adult male attribute seemed to me to be the ability to weld. Anybody could learn to saw and hammer wood, but to be able to cut metal apart and stick it back together—any way you wanted it—that would really be something. I tried welding a couple of times, and it was every bit as difficult as I'd imagined.

How is it, I ask myself, as I contemplate some dubious lash-up or other, that I have grown from a scrawny adolescent to this anxious, sometimes doddering, old fool without a single way-station of confidence and security along the way? I've rebuilt a couple of automobile engines, competed athletically in national championships, skied large mountains and driven racing cars, fathered children, written books. And all of it (well, not the children) in pursuit of some nebulous adulthood that retreats ahead of me, never getting a step closer. At some idiotic level I seem to believe there is a single act I can perform, at the end of which I'll come out with the word "competent" stamped on my forehead. When it comes to adulthood, I am— at fifty-four—like the erstwhile maiden on the morning after, staring in the mirror to see if the change in her status has registered in her eyes.

On one occasion only did I ever succeed in out-rigging my stepfather. We were driving a winch truck across an open field, and got stuck in a hidden ditch. Well, let's dig it out, Ott said, handing me a shovel and grabbing one himself. We began digging. It was a hellishly hot Texas afternoon. There was a large pecan tree thirty yards away. I kept looking at it and looking back at him, unable to believe he wasn't making the connection. After we'd dug for awhile, and he'd made one unsuccessful attempt to drive the truck out, I asked him if the cable on the winch wouldn't reach the tree. It was one of the more rewarding moments of my youth. He looked at me as if I were a stranger trying to hand him a fifty-dollar bill. "Guess we could try," he finally said, and reeled off the cable, wrapped it around the tree, and hauled the truck out of the ditch in about forty-five seconds. He was silent the rest of the way across the field, while I choked back grins. He never mentioned it again. It was my largest, maybe my only, triumph over him, and I remember it now, forty years later, as vividly as if it were yesterday.

In suggesting a solution to the problem with the truck, I was only trying to be smart enough to be accepted into, take part in, the world of rigging. Ott's world. But at the time, I didn't think of it as being smart, I thought I was just trying to get out of the work of shoveling out the truck by hand.

———

Reasonable men would agree, after one or two of those abortive attempts to raise Charybdis, that a more ingenious level of engineering was called for, but I was working by myself, with no one against whom to test ideas, let alone to suggest better ones. So I soldiered on—"unthinkingly" doesn't say it by half—on the idiotic assumption that on one of these hare-brained attempts I would manage to balance the stone all the way up to its tip-over point, and it would slide neatly into the hole. As its sister, on the other side of the driveway, had done, with two of us to guide it.

It was a project that kept getting stupider the closer I got to that goal. The higher the stone rose, the more I was forced to work underneath it. I would carefully test the balance of the stone on its props and then gingerly reach under, removing and replacing the jack as quickly as possible. There was a style of snatching to it, reminding me of the child's game played with a different kind of jack: throw a small rubber ball into the air, and, with quick hands, try to accomplish as much as possible before it comes down again. The phrase "jaws of death" kept popping into my mind, as I scrambled around on my knees after suitable props and wedges, one hand attempting to balance the stone. "Stupidest thing I've ever done," I would say as I danced out of the way of flying construction equipment, and kept right on doing it. I couldn't believe I was continuing; I believe it even less now, thinking back on that silly afternoon.

Afterward, I didn't sleep much that night. I've lain awake a few early morning hours since, thinking of that stone and the great *whump!* with which it kept smashing back into the earth each time I dropped it. Thinking of what would have happened if my leg, for instance, had been under it. I would have been unable to get it out, home alone, lying in the hot sun for a few hours. Trying to pry it up enough to drag the leg out, and having it slip and fall again on the already mangled limb. Repeating to myself: foolish. Foolish. Foolish. Why did I keep trying to do it by myself? Just because it was so easy, so seductive, to stick the end of a pry bar under the edge of the stone and lift it that first few inches?

When, after much staring, you get a stone to fit, there is a moment of epiphany. You see, with a flutter of hope, a stone with a shape that seems to match the shape of the hole you want to fill; you flip it over to the wall and lever it up into place; it goes, it fits, it fills the space nicely. You get a small rush of pleasure, of closure. ("Get *in* it," you say.) It encourages you to stare harder, looking for the next one.

I wrestle a dead branch away from the dogs and throw it aside, into the woods. It hits a tree exactly right and positively explodes, with a clean *crack!*, the dried-out dead wood smacking into the tree perfectly, some weak point in its wood fibers caught precisely at the point of impact. There is a strange small spike of pleasure in the cleanness of that snap. Splitting maple cordwood, the driven axe cleaving across the rings at just the right angle to make the log pop open, is an even more satisfying version of the same appropriateness of force. If I can remember, that is, not to go at log-splitting off balance, in a flurry, without slowing to look for the grain. Determined only to get this "unpleasant" work over with. (I love splitting wood, so long as I don't have to.) Trying to drive the maul in when the log is already toppling over, or to drive the wedge into rubbery wet heartwood that just spits it out again. There's nothing quite so unsatisfactory as having the log spit the wedge out again. It's the exact anti-sensation to the pleasure of a clean split.

There is a smaller rush of pleasure, but pleasure nonetheless, when you lift a heavy weight past the sticking place, when to continue the lift suddenly requires less, rather than more, force. There is also the moment when you break a heavy stone loose, when it's stuck, frozen in place, and you find a place to stick a pry bar under it, and put some force on the bar, and feel that first break, that *give* of movement. When you put a wrench on a nut and strain at it, and feel—with your muscles, you can't see it—that first give. Movement. (If you're not in motion, you can't change direction.)

Or when you stop staring pointlessly at the world, or gibbering at yourself in your head, or whatever distracting thing it is that you're doing, and actually see something. See *into* the behavior of an animal or the landscape or the problem at hand. I sell myself on the idea of rhythm, of dance, but I'm not good at those pleasures, I go sliding past them. It is when things stop that counts. (As in the poem: it's the stop—by the woods, on the snowy evening—isn't it?) It is when I am finally stopped, when the sentence falls right, when what I'm trying to say finally comes off my tongue, when I understand what someone is saying to me, when the pieces fall together and what was muddy confusion is suddenly clear: the eureka moment, when some conglomeration of ideas comes together for you, that otherwise, until then, you were unable to link. A connection made that you can't explain, that just . . . furthers you, somehow.

I used to have a wonderful quote about this moment pinned above my desk, but I lost it. Insert your own wonderful quote here. Mine was about that moment before which all is confusion and despair, and after which things suddenly become clear and there's never going to be any confusion anymore. It doesn't work out that way, of course, but the moment when you think it will is worth preserving. It is what I work for, I think.

The physical epiphanies available in working with wood and metal and stone are no different from those other little instants when some flicker of truth comes in. When the information from some sense organ or other succeeds in breaking through. I always thought these moments were supposed to be intellectual, the product of pure abstract thought. But they come to us through the sense organs. It was the taste of the apple, I think, that flipped us out of Eden, into the world.

———

I finally jacked and tilted the stone well past the point at which there was any doubt about being able to muscle it into the hole, and in the end brought it so near the point of balance that I could shove it into place with one hand. End of story, Scylla and Charybdis in place. That was on a Wednesday; on Friday I met Willy for lunch, and as I slid into the booth and saw his smiling face, I realized—with a jolt comprised of shock, grinning stupidity, and pure hopelessness—that I should have built a tripod.

When I first started talking about wall-building, Willy had wondered whether I wouldn't be using tripods a lot. I knew what he was talking about immediately—the back yards of my

youth had been dotted with timber tripods, used to pull the
engines out of soon-to-be-derelict automobiles. You cut three
stout timbers, six inches or so in diameter and twelve or fifteen
feet long, and chain their top ends together, tepee style. From
the chain you hang a block and tackle or other lifting device.
Pure-dee rigging: lift a thousand pounds, straight up, in com-
parative ease and safety.

I'd resisted Willy's suggestion because, in my head, anyway,
the occasion for a straight lift seldom occurred—at least not
graphically enough for me to recognize it. Besides, say I located
a good stone somewhere that was too large to lift or lever into
my wagon: once I had the damned thing in the air, hanging
from a tripod, wouldn't the legs get in the way of my wagon
so I couldn't get it under the stone? And other red herrings.
(Build the tripod taller, you jerk, Willy could have explained,
if I'd chosen to discuss it with him.)

The time that Willy suggested I might someday want to use
a tripod was also the time he'd told me about his lumberman
friend who had this talent for walking around the problem until
he saw the solution. Romantic logging tales, I had thought at
the time. But walking around the problem was just what I
hadn't done with Charybdis. My mental set had frozen with
the concept of pushing up from below—jacking—instead of
pulling from above. I didn't have a point from which to lift; I
needed a skyhook, a.k.a. a tripod. Everything I needed was
within fifty yards of where I worked—timber at the edge of the
woods, block and tackle in the garage. But I never walked
around and looked at the thing hard enough. I just kept clawing
at it, prying away and stuffing things under it, figuring any
minute now something was going to give in. Hoping it wouldn't
be my back, or my skull.

———

The good old boys back home usually adopt the concept of the tripod after one of their number knocks his car off the jack and drops it on himself. Someone was always doing that, or having a car fall off a grease rack, or a tractor flip over on him. Discussion of these fatalities filled the air around a lot of domino games. Any damned fool ought to know better than that.

My stubbornness is a majestic edifice. If I'd killed myself out of stupidity, it would really have been Willy's fault for suggesting the tripod in the first place, thereby automatically excluding it from consideration as a solution. Erasing it from my mind. Well, if I am stubborn toward others' good counsel, it is as nothing to how I treat my own best advice. Thinking back about these matters sends me out to take a walk around the two vertical stones that still mark the head of my driveway. See if I can't dope out the precise spot to stick a crowbar underneath my ego, in hopes of finding the leverage to pry that sucker out of the *way*, you know?

F A L L

P A R T   I I I

[9]

S E P T E M B E R :

W I L L Y

The maple leaves outside my window are still bright green, but their stems are already turning yellow, on the way to red. I never noticed that before: the colors in the fall foliage must work their way outward from stem to tip. Of course. The abscission layer, which forms in autumn and cuts off the supply of sap to the leaf, must form at the twig end; otherwise, when the leaves fell, they wouldn't still have stems on them, would they? The stems would stay on the tree, leaving it looking not so much bare as porcupinish.

When I look directly down at the grass as I mow, I am now beginning to be teased by the red end of the spectrum—again, not directly discernible but at the corner of my eye, spring's subliminal tints beginning to come back the other way. Here and there a single maple bough has gone bright yellow, or red, in a sea of green; oh, it's just diseased, Chris and I always say to each other. Doesn't mean anything yet. But hawks are tumbling at great heights over the valley, and smaller birds are beginning to flock. Every stalk has a seedhead on it. In the next field over, the dogs and I thrash through a patch of spotted touch-me-not, the pods popping and scattering on contact, spewing seeds every which way, making me think at first that we're walking through a swarm of grasshoppers. Putting new seed down now, to lay under the snow for next year.

On a cloudy day in the woods, the light swells and darkens again, pulling my mood along with it. At the top of the loop, the light comes from a different, lower place than a month ago. The air turns cool the moment the sun goes out of it. Fall *is* on the way, too damned early this year too. Every sign of it, lovely and sad, is keyed in some way to the changing angle of the light. A whole damned season, kicked off by nothing more than variations in the attitude of arrival of photons from the sun.

Making yellow creep up the maple stems outside my window. I look up at the forest on the hill and imagine I can hear, inside all those stems, a zillion little doors clanging shut. Shutters pulled in, shades rattling down. Tree to leaf: you're beautiful, but you're history. You're archives. You just got a promotion: your new job is *mulch*.

Willy brings over his two-man saw, to help me take down the scary fourteen-inch beech that is blocking the gap between the two lower fields. He's also brought an axe, wedges, a sledge, a small machete for brambles; to this armamentarium I add my chainsaw—in case of emergency—and a scythe and another axe, and we drive his pick-up down to the gap. Later I will walk back for the crowbar and chain we forgot.

We circle the intended victim on foot, clearing things, redistributing an old brushpile that is in the way. We're searching not only for good footing and room to swing our elbows but

also, at Willy's suggestion, for the widest possible assortment
of escape routes, for when the tree starts coming down. There's
a snag that has to be removed first, a long-dead eight-inch pine
standing precariously on a rotten base, almost punky enough
to be pushed over by hand, but entangled, at the top, with
other trees. It suggests the possibility that some large and heavy
upper part could break off and fall on us, reminding us why
forest workers wear hard-hats, which we also didn't bring.
Willy chops it down, grunting on the first few strokes at the
unfamiliarity of swinging an axe again. It's been a long time.
When the snag crashes down it shatters, in its rottenness, into
several parts.

Time to cut down the tree we came for. It leans out into the
clearing at a fifty-degree angle, but appears to be solid and
sound, with no surprises hidden away beneath its bark—and
no wasp nests in its branches. (When I was clearing the original
gap, I'd been cutting away for a couple of hours before I noticed
a full-grown porcupine overhead, watching me from the crown
of a tree that I was on the point of felling. That time I'd
remembered to wear a hard-hat, but it didn't feel like adequate
protection against falling porcupines.) Willy and I discuss angles and approaches; we've talked about these matters in the
past, and I notice a certain respectful competition between us
to see who can be the most careful, the most safety-minded,
in sizing up the task. At the angle this tree leans, we agree,
there's absolutely no question about where, within a very few
degrees of arc, it is going to fall. We're going to have very
little to say about that.

This robs the occasion of its largest intellectual challenge.
I'd joked beforehand that perhaps we should each place a stake
where we thought the tree would fall, and see whose stake
came closest to being driven further into the ground. The rules

for aiming a falling tree are well established. (Carrying them out, though—requiring skills—can be another matter.) You cut a wedge-shaped notch on the side toward which you want the tree to fall. You align this notch so the straight line of its deepest edge is at a right angle to the line on which you want the trunk of the tree to land. Then you make a felling cut from the other side, aligned parallel with but slightly above the back of the notch. The object is to cut through to just above the notch, leaving a one-inch hinge. Before the tree gets unstable, you drive a wedge into the felling cut behind the saw. When you're within about an inch of the original notch you should be able to push the tree over to start its fall; if you can't, driving the wedge deeper will usually do the job. Or you can use the crowbar we forgot to bring.

I had avoided cutting this particular tree with the chainsaw because it already leaned so far that it obviously would start to sag, trapping my saw, as soon as I began cutting a notch on the underside. It also looked as if it might want to twist, unpredictably, as it fell. I wasn't sure how to proceed. The (hand-powered) two-man saw, slower and more manageable, seemed safer. What was true for the chainsaw was true for the two-man saw, though, and we decided there was no point in trying to cut the notch on the underside. There was nothing to do but begin with a felling cut on the side away from the fall.

So we started working with the two-man saw—called, in earlier times, a misery whip. It is a device that takes some getting on to, and to tell the truth I'm not sure I ever really did. To leave a minimally disruptive stump, we were trying to cut the tree low to the ground, which meant an awkward working position—on our knees—to start with. Just about any way I could find to work positioned me so the sawteeth threatened to cut across the flesh of my thigh as well as the trunk of the tree, which kept me nervously shifting my stance. Willy's arms are short, mine long, which confused the issue of length of stroke. It was frustrating, which may have been exactly what Willy had meant when he said that two-man sawing was an experience I shouldn't miss.

For the first few inches of the cut we were still in the muscle of the bole that Charlie Gray used to talk about. Willy explained the term: it is the area where the circumference of the tree is still lumpy, convexly scalloped, with the great tubes of wood fiber feeding up from the roots. Once you get past this lumpy area—or if you make your cut above it, further up the trunk—you're in the "clear." As we cut deeper we would get into the clear, Willy said, and the saw would begin to work better. It did.

I'm finally learning to warm up for work, not with formal calisthenics but just an easier, more gingerly way of moving, a careful avoidance of hard effort or sudden load until I've been at it awhile. Beginning to sweat is the sign, of course, indicating that the self-generated heat that wets the outside of the muscle has also lubricated the inside. Before I began investigating athletics, I would often go for months without ever breaking a sweat, and when I did would find its wetness shocking. There are complex formulas for how much exercise one should get—so many minutes at such and such a heart-rate so many times a week. The numbers, handed down by experts, are generally regarded as gospel, but have been snatched, I believe, from air. Breaking a sweat is easier to remember.

There's a complete collection of these formulas in my change-or-die file. Most of the contents of that file are programmatic in nature, schemes designed by exercise scientists, health professionals, and other bureaucrats of well-being. To the extent that the programs are physiological in their approach, and that one is patient in their application, they seem to work, and to work about equally well, demonstrating that some kinds of change are possible. None of them, so far, has been very effective against the scurrying in my head. My assumption is that that is nonphysiological.

But then I have a physiological bias. Prayer, I think, might work as well. Every time you lift a stone, repeat the phrase "God, please make it lighter." Have faith, keep lifting, and eleven and a half days later, by God, the stones will be lighter. Or you'll be stronger, same thing. Here might be a physiology of prayer. Whether it is God that is responding to the repeated entreaty or physiology that is responding to the repeated stress is open to interpretation, but the resulting strength gain is actually schedulable. It operates on a twenty-one-day cycle. At eleven and a half days, you've begun to accommodate to the load; after twenty-one days, if you want to continue to gain, you have to increase it. Pick up bigger stones. These physiological details are from my file folder. In the trade they are known as cocktail facts.

The mills of physiological change also grind exceeding slow, and exceeding small. If change is to be bound into place, it must take place at the level of the cell; one wrenches oneself along a micromillimeter, a molecule at a time. It would be so much easier to skip the physiology and just, you know, *change*. Make the decision and then do it. My posture is bad, my shoulders slump; why don't I just stand up straight, the way my mother always told me? Bypass the cells: change by sloganeering. There's some of that in the file folder too. I'm not sure I understand why it never works. There's a note taped to my word processor that says "Stop killing snakes," but I never notice it anymore.

I have a problem with listening. The first time Willy mentioned a tree's muscle to me was when he was telling me about Charlie Gray, how Charlie had taught him to see the muscle in the wood. I'd let the term pass, in part wanting Willy to think that guys like me knew all about things like that, in part dismissing it as folklore, or nonsense—this seeing into trees and anthropomorphizing their structure. I don't know why I don't ask the obvious question at the appropriate time. This time I did ask, and saw immediately that this muscle business referred to a real, discernible structure. I didn't figure out why it was harder to saw until much later. It's simply tougher. The fibers, in each of those muscular lumps that come up from the roots, are arranged in tight concentric circles, so you're sawing grain that goes every which way. Deeper inside, where there is only one set of concentric circles to cut across, everything is more uniform, aligned. Clear. The saw goes more smoothly.

As we sawed away, more sawdust was piling up on Willy's side of the tree than on mine, for reasons I could not discern. I figured this was from some inadequacy or lack of effort on my part; gentlemanly Willy said it was only gravity, my side being on higher ground. (But switching sides didn't help.) Part of my problem was that I kept wanting to *saw* the goddamned thing, put some force into it, but you can't do that. If you get ahead of your partner and try to drive the saw back to him, the blade will bow and then bind in the cut. Your partner has to pull the blade back. The secret seems to be to do it all lightly, keeping the blade aligned and letting the saw do the work. When the cut begins to get out of alignment, changing the angle at which the saw works, you can pull it back— "cutting into your corner," Willy called it. The ideal, though, is to keep the blade square to the cut, with even pressure on it. When you get it going good the saw will indeed start to sing to you, sliding back and forth with what seems like no effort at all. But if it is so effortless, why did I have to get Willy to stop every couple of minutes to give me a chance to blow? (Why else would they call it a misery whip?)

After a while there was a loud crack as the weakened tree, leaning even farther, began splitting lengthwise up the trunk. Geometry immediately set in: the crack cocked open the upper surface of the cut, taking up some of its space, binding the saw. We stopped and talked things over. Couldn't figure out anything to do but continue, working our way haltingly past the tendency of the saw to bind. Eventually there came a second loud crack, and we had to withdraw the saw and widen the cut with an axe—not easy, as our accuracy with axes had not been tested in the previous ten or fifteen years.

With the third loud crack the tree fell, majestically enough, although by then it leaned so sharply that it didn't have far to fall. It settled into the ground still seriously fouled at the stump, sawed two-thirds through and broken the rest of the way, the broken joint—two feet higher than the cut itself—a twisted tangle of wood fibers. Instead of a one-inch hinge, we had one that was a third of the trunk in thickness. It was definitely not the clean job you wanted when sawing down a tree, leaving a few thousand pounds of wet green trunk hawsered to the stump with twisted wood. Hard to release that kind of pressure, hard to get the whole thing clear. Damn. No fault of the two-man saw, but . . . Oh, *I* get it (smacking forehead), *that's* why you cut that first notch. When you can.

———

As Willy and I worked, we didn't talk a great deal—surprising, as we tend to gibber at each other fairly energetically under less preoccupying circumstances. I did, however, make a few observations. Maybe even several. I seem to feel compelled to do that around Willy, perhaps because he actually knows actual things. Having spent his boyhood (and several years more) around here, he knows the bugs and flowers and rocks, the names of things and their habits. He doesn't have the culture-warp that I am fighting through; he's my connection to a proper alignment with this particular local physical world.

Willy is also a writer. It occurs to me that we might have gone at this work poetically, stopping to wax lyrical, straining to top each other in insight and perception and graceful analysis. Excepting my observations, we avoided that. We also avoided the style favored by the men I worked with in my youth, the Southwestern, or taciturn, way: just doing the work without discussing it, leaving it to the other guy to dope out what you're after, what needs doing next. I notice both these styles contain an element of masculine competitiveness. Instead, we just worked it out, discussing our way through it the best way we could. That was nice.

Willy did reflect that he wished he did more of this kind of thing, he enjoyed it so, and had a great deal of it to do on his place, but was hard pressed to make himself take the time. On the other hand, he said, he also really enjoyed writing, an extremely time-intensive line of work. I quoted Annie Dillard at him—"you do what you do out of your private passion for the thing itself"—but we otherwise managed to eschew writerliness. To, I think, our mutual relief.

Afterward, as he was leaving, Willy remembered, somewhat wistfully, how for several adolescent years he had kept himself feeling good, and feeling good about himself, by doing that sort of work. How he missed it. Those were years when he attended boarding school, not altogether willingly, while his parents traipsed the halls of power and prestige elsewhere. I think he also learned a lot about that kind of work directly from his late father, who was also a writer, and who also got great personal satisfaction out of working away at the physical world. But Willy talks more, on these occasions, about Charlie Gray.

Willy is more analytical than I am, I think. He is inclined to know the rules, to spell out and understand the techniques in his own head (and therefore to be able to teach them), perhaps because he learned them that way himself. Ott, my principal instructor in these matters, whose Southwestern style of work is referred to above, never opened his mouth about how you did anything, only about what you did: put that board there, without a word about how you got it there or held it securely in place. No rules, just plans. (A saw? It was just this implement, you picked it up and pushed it back and forth across the wood. Eventually it would work, never mind learning how to make it go easier, or cut more accurately.) As a result of that, perhaps, I go at things in more of a fit-and-try, right-brained way, getting them by feel and visual image rather than outlined procedures. This difference between Willy and me is not cut and dried, these are not rigid divisions, but I think he leans one way and I the other. My approach precludes passing anything on.

———

There is surely a kind of physical lyricism to be obtained in working with a two-man saw, but I'm not sure we reached it. We didn't do it long enough to lodge it in my brain; I didn't dream, that night, of operating a two-man saw, as often happens when I've done some other repetitive physical task, the rhythm seeping up to the surface of sleep. Stone work does, sometimes, get into my sleep; the two-man saw didn't. My loss.

But the saw and the other large hand tools did stir up a

queer atavistic mood, filling my head with fringed buckskin, yoked oxen—or the movie versions, anyway. I paused once when using the axe, and let the handle slip lightly down through my hand, catching it at the wonderful little surprise six-gun curl at the end. When that lip snugged up against my little finger, the ghost of some movie gun-fighter tip-toed across my grave—Joel McCrea, I believe it was—and I almost reached with the other hand to swing back the saloon door. I mentioned this funny flicker of image to Willy; he immediately demonstrated how, as a kid, that same wristy heft of the axe would absolutely force him to swing it up, cock it behind his ear, and throw it at a nearby tree trunk. A lumberjack in an Errol Flynn movie. He stopped short, in his demonstration, of actually heaving it, and I was relieved at that, too. I had this further image of two middle-aged men giving themselves up to those fantasies, standing at the edge of a clearing in the woods, throwing axes at trees until we'd littered the forest floor with gouged-out chunks of beech, birch, maple, and broken axe handles, if not gobbets of flesh.

Instead, we chopped the tree loose and levered it off its splintered stump, then sawed a couple of clear six-foot lengths off the trunk for firewood. Working upright on a horizontal log, the saw did begin to sing a bit more sweetly, giving a hint of how, if you got good enough at it, such work might turn hypnotic. I have a friend who was an Olympic rower, whose eyes soften when he talks about "swing." That's what oarsmen call that moment when all eight oars are truly in sync, and the boat begins to leap and drive ahead, temporarily more than the sum of its parts. I think something like that could happen with two people sawing; it is timing, not effort, that does it, though, and I did not master it. The thing is there, I think—you keep getting hints of its existence—but we were too old and misaligned to pick up its rhythms that quickly. The misery whip turned out to be a bit of a tease.

————

When Marty and I raised the gate stone, we worked closely in concert, but when it came to finishing off the remaining gap in the wall, we weren't collaborating so much as doing the same work side by side. (We didn't have to collaborate, the stones weren't that large.) We worked fast and hard, pushing to get through, throwing stones on pretty much willy-nilly: Marty trying to get done, I suppose, and I, catching urgency from him, trying to release him from ancient obligations. If you look at the wall now you can see the patch that the two of us put in. That stretch has the same dimensions, is as tall and wide as the rest of the wall, but you can make out our insert, a faint saddle in the wall where the texture changes. The stones there are placed differently than the stones to either side. When Marty asked for a principle by which to place the stones, I couldn't give him one (and still can't). It turns out, though, that there is, in the stacking of stones, if not an expressible working principle then at least a personal signature. I wouldn't have known it existed if Marty hadn't joined me in the work.

Or maybe personal signature is overdignifying it; maybe it's simply a change of pace, a different speed of working, written into the wall. For months afterward I would look at that patch and think I ought to take it out, replace the stones more tightly, to preserve the wall's visual unity. But I've come to like the idea of a piece of my son's work, of our mutual work in concert, in the wall. It's a memento of a nice day in our lives.

With a two-man saw, there's not much question about matching pace. The two of you are tied together on each end of a single appliance, forcing accommodation. When you get the saw going right, your principal responsibility is, in a sense, simply to pull the other guy's arms back out straight, so he's in position to start the next stroke. Maybe that is what is so satisfying about it. Now that I think of it, the two-man saw cuts on the pull, like a Japanese handsaw. American handsaws cut on the push. This may be the part that takes getting on to. It's a bigger difference than I'd ever have thought.

There were a couple more of those six-foot lengths of firewood to take, but we ran out of time and energy. Enough. It hadn't been the slickest tree-felling in history, but the problems that our mistakes had generated were small ones, and interesting in themselves, modestly challenging in their solutions. We weren't entirely competent yet (or, in Willy's case, again) as loggers, but that didn't make us bad people. The requisite skills could even conceivably be (re)acquired, if our old bodies held out. I learned a dozen things about woods work that I'd never thought of before. The tree was safely down, no longer nagging at the corner of my attention. At least some of the wood wouldn't go to waste.

We'd carefully planned the whole operation to end at cocktail time, of course. If we had been an authentic woods crew, I suppose we should have finished up with cans of beer, leaning on the fender of Willy's truck. In fact we are both mostly sedentary rural homeowners, mostly nervous about keeping up our property, and besides, we've acquired other tastes. There were cushioned chairs on the porch, and a wider assortment of drink. I noticed that the pleasures of the cool circle of sweat on the collar, the gradual relaxation of quivering muscles, did not diminish, and were not diminished by, the very different pleasure of some very dry gin.

EQUINOX:
REALIGNMENT

Damn March, bless September: Just as winter hung on then, summer lingers now, holding off the fall. We get hints—green growth has slowed sharply, the occasional passing weather front is a little cooler—but summer is still with us. The pond stays swimmable. In fact it is warmer now than it was in July: the spring water that fills it is still losing its chill, never mind that the air temperature is changing in the opposite direction. (Late June, with the longest days and the most sun, is not the hottest time of year, nor is late December's shortest day the coldest. Nature's water content always drags the seasons along a month or so behind the movements of the planet. This is not an original observation; a biologist explained the physics of it to me.)

The equinox arrives crisply, with rarefied air and a blindingly glorious, bright blue sky, and by ten o'clock I am at my wall, determinedly working in nothing but shorts and sneakers—a little chilly but wanting the air on my skin, conscious that I'll be bundling up again before long. A butterfly lands on the bridge of my nose as I work. Woops, it isn't a butterfly, but whatever it is is definitely in love with me. Fall is a wacky time for wildlife. And for the dogs and cats. And me. I begin to find the equinoctial splendor frustrating: pay attention to the rocks and lose the day, pay attention to the day and lose the rocks. I keep flipping back and forth across that threshold— focusing down, completely absorbed with the work, and then my attention drawn back up and out to the sky, air, light. Trying to cram it all in, nail down this stupendous day. Maybe it's not just the coming of fall: hell, I may not get too many more days like this in . . . my lifetime. Gulp. Moments later stone work has been abandoned, and I am sitting at the top of the pasture above the house, trying to see everything, everything. My fifty-fifth birthday, six weeks away, surely marks at least the late August, if not early September, of my life. A fact like that has me paying a little different kind of attention to the arrival of this particular autumn.

My eye is caught by a swirl of bugs in the brilliant sun, pulling each other into tight vertical circles in a peculiar dipping, darting dance. I have no idea what kind of bugs they are, but they seem to have no other business than to make a swirling disk of bugness over some indeterminate spot halfway up the hill. Then my vision manages to break through that activity to the blue shadow of the woods at the periphery of the field, hitting me over the head with the enormous volume of air space over the hillside. The angle of the sun backlights these small insects, making them visible, in the same way a beam lights up dust motes, or smoke. It also highlights floating milkweed seeds, and spider webs, and then I realize the air is full of protein, full of mass, there are all these chunks and bits floating around in it (on this perfectly clear, still day), and the huge distance is a sea of living bodies, whirling around in all the empty space. The image that occurs to me is the one astronomers use to describe an expanding universe: raisins in a rising cake; bugs as stars, as planets, rushing away from each other in all directions. The image is faulty, of course; there's no expansion to it, it's only a whirling dance. But then what isn't?

———

Our house, according to the contour map, is 1,130 feet above sea level; the top of the field where I sit is about 1,200 feet, the high point on the loop at 1,460, the height of land just beyond our property at 1,510. Sea level is 120 miles to the east, in Boston Harbor. The hills around here—quite gentle, after the mountains of New Hampshire—are the foothills of a low range called the Hoosacs, which are the foothills of the Berkshires, which in turn are foothills of the Green Mountains of Vermont. Twenty miles to the west and north, tucked away in the corner bordered by New York and Vermont, is Mt. Greylock—at 3,491 feet, the highest point in Massachusetts.

At the winter solstice, when it is most precious, sunlight first touches our place on the northwesternmost corner of the lower field, at about eight-fifteen; it leaves from the northeasternmost corner of the adjoining lower field well before three-thirty in the afternoon. (Cutting the gap between the two fields helped make these observations possible.) At the summer solstice—in fact at least from equinox to equinox—the sun has moved around so that the light touches first the high point of the property. The entire hillside is north-facing, which is significant. Leaving our deep valley in New Hampshire, we longed for a sunny, south-facing hill, but didn't find one, found this place instead and fell in love with it. It has worked out fine, but the feel of the place is heavily influenced by its northern orientation. It holds the snow. (Ski-resort developers seek out northeast exposures.) The snow stays longest where the north wind packs it in against the treeline at the top of the fields and below the steeper pitches of the hill. Across the valley, in early spring, we will see brown hillsides toasting in the sun while we are still buried. We are house-bound a week or two later than some of our neighbors.

The hillside itself is an irregular north-northeast plane; the house sits two-thirds of the way down, on a knoll that pops out of the slope and gives the house a level landing place. There are two fields below, and one above the house, where I sit now in the September sun. Between me and the house there is a textbook definition of a swale, in which sits the shallow well that is our water supply. The swale diverts the water coming down off the hill, in a minor run-off to the northeast and to the pond to the southwest. Above me, a mix of trashy hemlocks cuts like a chevron across the hill's face, following the shoulders of the rocky outcrops of east-west bedding planes. Near the top there's a small gorge running on a north-south line close to one edge of the property; the hill itself is steep there, and the sides of the gorge much steeper. Grapevines have entangled the hemlocks and pulled the tops down into the gorge. It's a mess. The vines don't bear fruit and are pestiferous, but cutting only stimulates them; to remove them requires poisons and a chemical-injecting axe, and we haven't found the resolve to take that harsh step. Blackberries, as I have mentioned, spring up wherever the forest canopy is penetrated. Alders take over the wet spots. This is the way this particular piece of land works. Attempts to clear out alders are always futile. Perhaps if I drained the wet spots I'd have better luck.

––––––––

Yesterday was, ceremonially, our last canoe trip of the year. The Hoosacs are split by the Deerfield River, which tumbles down from Vermont, hooks a left somewhere near the nuclear plant in Rowe, and then meets up with the broad Connecticut twenty miles or so to the east. Willy and his wife, Liz, an accomplished poet, introduced us to the pleasures of floating down the Deerfield in the summertime. There are several stretches that allow an easy put-in and take-out, even with picnic basket and cooler. It's a good idea to phone the appropriate upstream dam to find out what level of flow to expect. When the water is high, as it was for this trip, canoeing is fine; when it's low, you end up wading much of the way, dragging the canoe. A wet-walk, Willy calls it; inflatables are then a better solution.

Whatever the vessel, it is an entirely undemanding sport, a lazy few hours of drifting, swimming in the deep holes (some of which have rope swings), picnicking on islands. We float along looking for birds; here and there along the bank there's usually a mother duck with flock of ducklings, swimming in formation, and we are torn between wanting to tiptoe quietly past and, as always in nature, the urge to go get a closer look. On the right kind of summer day, you bake in your canoe for awhile—or even work up a little sweat paddling it—then slip over the side and get cool again, anytime you want. The smells of the river always remind me of my father, the fly fisherman.

We didn't do much swimming yesterday: a cool front was passing through (responsible for today's atmospheric brilliance), accompanied by a brisk north breeze. The river was warm enough, but the air, when you climbed out again, was not. Not swimming did not significantly diminish the pleasures of the trip. (The Deerfield stays a little warmer, by the way, for going by the nuclear plant at Rowe, which borrows it briefly for cooling purposes. We didn't know this at first, and it gave us a peculiar jolt when we found out. Okay, maybe nuclear power is every bit as safe as they claim, but that doesn't prevent the quiet question that rises in the back of my mind each time I slide into the river for a swim. And I wouldn't eat one of its fish.)

Chris and I went on one or two of these trips as guests, then bought a canoe of our own and set about learning to use it. I had done some canoeing in my youth, Chris hadn't. Like the two-man saw, a canoe requires a certain agreement about the application of force. Two paddlers generate very different forces from one. If you learn to paddle in the stern and then switch to the bow, the steering strokes seem to accomplish rather the opposite of your intent, and vice versa. We practiced in our pond at home a time or two, but with no current and ten or twelve strokes between one shore and the next, we didn't learn a great deal. In the river, we always find ourselves working harder at steering, at keeping our craft in control, than perhaps we need to.

We just want a float; why are we working away at it so? Our canoeing is not white-water adventure. There are ripples here and there that are best taken straight on (and we've dumped ourselves a time or two when we haven't been paying attention), but the Deerfield is mostly placid, and which side of the river you happen to be on, or where you go next, makes little difference. The river is going exactly where you want eventually to go, which is to the place where you left the second car.

Might as well drift. Still, we keep applying force, driving the thing ahead. Can't seem to stop. Why is this? What's the hurry, Mr. Urgency?

———

From the top of the pasture I try to see clearly the house and the knoll it sits on, three hundred yards away. Not that the view is obstructed: I've just seen it too many times and gotten used to it, and still never grasped it well enough to satisfy me. I've studied the maps and the surveyor's plat, noted down the appropriate numbers, but I'm teased by the certainty that there is a different kind of triangulation to be acquired—outside the bureaucracy of alignment—if only I can unlock it. Despite living here for eight years, working on the place, walking it, enjoying it daily, it still won't pin down for me. I must still be trying to crank the points of the compass into place.

The moment I make the decision to try to see the place more deeply, I start analyzing, picking out details, putting words on it. The only way I know to really see the place is to try to explain it, describe it as I would to someone else. As I would write about it. So I make notes, sitting in the sun on a gorgeous day while the dogs mess around the perimeter and occasionally stop back by to see if I'm doing anything interesting yet. This is not onerous duty.

Making notes, however, is frustrating. I don't get much practice at writing by hand, and do it with some difficulty. The notes are therefore boiled down to the absolute minimum, in words, even in symbols, that I will later be able to reconstruct. I should have learned shorthand or some other code, but didn't, which means devising a new code as I go, which splits the attention between devising the code and getting down the note itself. Besides, a certain self-consciousness sets in: just who the hell do I think I am, sitting on a hill making notes? This splits off another fragment of mental circuitry, an additional diversion from thinking about whatever it was that made me want to make a note in the first place. Meanwhile, all I really want to do—I swear it—is sit in the sun at the top of the pasture and enjoy the day. Stopping to make notes about the place, or the day, means losing my hold on that enjoyment. Ah, these realms of mind, these layers of attention.

My change-or-die file says that the work of paddling a canoe is aerobic and therefore good for us. Driving the thing forward is also fun. It feels good. The medium it moves in is wonderfully plastic and amenable, and the rhythm is hypnotic. I'm sure there's even a kind of swing to be achieved, in the eight-oared sense of the term, although we're far from that yet. It teases us, drawing us on; a bit of a bawd, the canoe, just like the two-man saw.

One of the nicer lessons of athletics is that there is genuine pleasure in effort, in a pace—if you can find it—that uses the muscles, kicks up the respiration, burns off a little of that frenetic energy that otherwise corrodes the soul. If, that is, you can do it without pushing over into the other craziness, as usually happens to me. I haven't learned to let go of the need to control, direct, keep the canoe (or anything else) pointed straight: the westernized, apollonian requirement that one master things, apply more power. I keep fiddling with the throttle.

Of course I *like* effort, but that is not a sufficient excuse. I like effortlessness more, or claim to. What I like most is the search for that, for the effortless way, for those little physical moments when it goes just right: epiphanies, again. What I like best about stone work is working at it slowly and carefully, figuring out how to get the stones and get them into place with never the strain of a heavy lift. I like trying to make stone work effortless, which is a satisfactorily impossible, and therefore endless, task. You can put a lot of effort into finding the effortless way.

———

The writer Annie Dillard says somewhere that she wants to plant a stake in time, the way a surveyor might stick one into the earth to mark a location. Looking for that quote, I run across this—about alignment—in *Teaching a Stone to Talk:* "The Pole of Relative Inaccessibility is 'that imaginary point on the Arctic Ocean farthest from land in any direction.'" (Obviously I had read this passage, but had forgotten it by the time I stumbled across that legend on my own map of the Antarctic.) "It's a navigator's paper point, contrived to console Arctic explorers who, after Peary and Henson reached the North Pole in 1909, had nowhere special to go." (I notice her definitions have a crispness that mine lack.)

Her comment continues: "The Absolute is the Pole of Relative Inaccessibility located in metaphysics. After all, one of the few things we know about the Absolute is that it is relatively inaccessible. It is that point of spirit farthest from every accessible point of spirit in all directions. Like the others, it is a Pole of the Most Trouble. It is also—I take this as a given—the pole of great price." Maybe I'm not working hard enough.

———

Zen Buddhism, I gather, is interested in matters such as these. When chopping wood and hauling water, Zen says, one should just chop wood, haul water. One of the ways I try to remember just to stack the stones is to tell myself what I'm doing as I do it. To tell myself my story, to relate it as it is going on. When I do, I always catch myself thinking, Gee, that's the way I wish I lived.

———

Ah, here's the Dillard quote, I had the wrong book (it's from *Pilgrim at Tinker Creek*): "This year I want to stick a net into time and say 'now,' as men plant flags on the ice and snow and say, 'here.'"

My note-taking, it strikes me, is nothing more than a pathetic attempt to plant a flag of my own in time. Or a way to think the compass back into place. (In a Mel Brooks interview, the questioner asks him how he gets his wonderful ideas. Well, like this, Brooks says, screwing up his face into a terrible grimace, grunting hard, then slapping himself on the forehead and smiling. That's how, he says.) Sitting at the top of the hill, I am struck by my happiness. I'm happy when my life goes along nicely, but I'm happier still when I'm pushing it along a little bit. Maybe the laying down of stones is trying to shove the compass back into place with physical effort.

The effort, in the moving of stones, is against gravity—a nostalgia for spheres, Descartes called it. Gravity also makes the river flow, among other things, for the canoe to float down (without our effortful paddling). In wintertime, looking across a wide expanse of smooth snow, I dream of skittering across its surface on unweighted skis. I long for less gravity, forgetting that the whole point, the pleasure, is in overcoming it. It is the alternate force, the bad opposite the good of physical movement: gravity as Satan. See also: free will, angels (free to fall). I forget that the appeal of those sensual sports comes specifically in contradicting gravity—making it easy, making it smooth, making it silky, getting the physics right. Getting the weight pushed up over center, so it will fall on the other side; getting gravity to work for you.

A stone wall is a tribute to gravity, in a sense, an acknowledgment of it. A temple to it. Maybe gravity is all the alignment one ever gets, and therefore all I ought to need. What more could one want, anyway, than the sure sense—right there, at any given moment for the noticing—of a straight line pointing toward the center of the earth?

[11]

OCTOBER:
HUES, ALSO
CRIES

Golden, golden, the woods are golden now. The days stretch on into Indian summer, the air gone plummy with woodsmoke and windfall apples, Stradivari air. The woods are golden and I walk in them every chance I get, ignoring the wall and other chores, and my work, ignoring also the old stone walls in the woods that nag at me, clamoring to be pulled down and carted back to the house. My wall, still unfinished but seventy feet long now, beckons to me far less than the woods do, far less than it did in spring and summer. To tell the truth, I don't have time for it; if I fulfill my responsibilities to myself and the dogs and the woods, if I follow the consistent impulse to bolt from the house and pick a spot on the ridgeline and bushwhack a straight line up to it, then wander over onto the back side on someone else's semi-abandoned land, stumbling over the uneven off-trail footing, wading ankle-deep in fallen leaves, staggering color-drunk through the great halls of maple, tracing sourceward the rivulets that come tumbling down over their dwindling creekbeds—trying to figure out what makes it so sweet to be up here in the woods, and why, once I get here, I don't want to come down again—I don't really have time for building walls. Not right now, in October.

Now I walk out of the house into the woods and am struck mostly by how right everything is, what nice balance there is in the design of the barks and grasses and even the way the twigs have fallen in the path. Nice distribution. Usually I am driven to manipulate things, trying to improve them somehow, get them exactly right. But not in October.

————

The foliage colors raise some interesting questions, sending me to the library. It's all chemicals, says the biochemistry text. Chlorophylls keep the leaves green while they are green, carotenoids—as in butter, corn, canary feathers—turn them yellow when the chlorophyll goes. Tannin adds the browns, the bronzes; something called anthocyanin turns leaves red if the sap of the plant is acidic, blue or purple if it is alkaline. Color is a substance, says the chemist. Funny how when you're a hammer, everything looks like a nail.

The physicist, on the other hand, says it all has to do with light. The leaves that look red are only reflecting that portion of the white light of the sun that is composed of waves on the order of thirty-two millionths of an inch long. Violet leaves reflect waves that are sixteen millionths of an inch long. All the other colors that autumn leaves (or anything else) can be, all the several million shades that the human eye can discern, are strung out along that sixteen millionths of an inch of difference: the total span of the visual portion of the electromagnetic spectrum. Yellow is smack in the middle, eight millionths of an inch away from red in one direction, eight millionths of an inch away from indigo in the other. I wouldn't have thought

I could discern eight millionths of an inch, but the physicists say it's as clear as the difference between, well, blue and yellow. Color is a distinction.

Then there's physiology, the uncanny capacity of the rods and cones of the eye to take these substances and distinctions and somehow turn them into the maelstrom of sensation that staggers me when I step out the door. Actually, the rods have nothing to do with it; only the cones deal with color, according to the books. Nobody knows quite how. The most popular theory posits three types of cone, one of which responds better to red, one to green, the third to violet. The various hues are perceived by combinations of response; when all three types are equally stimulated, the color white is perceived. By the eye, or the brain. Or the consciousness that operates the eye and the brain. Or the consciousness that is operated by the eye and brain.

Color, then, isn't a substance or a distinction but a pattern of nerve impulses—at least until it gets to the consciousness. "The eye is a device by which the energy of a light pattern is converted into the energy of a nerve impulse that is conducted by the optic nerve to the visual cortex of the brain for interpretation as a visual image," says Sigmund Grollman, in *The Human Body*. That's all fine and good, except for the interpretation part: electromagnetic vibrations into nerve signals, yes, but how do we turn nerve signals into whatever it is that makes this glory explode in our heads when we step outdoors into a hardwood forest in the fall? Funny how science inevitably comes bumping to a stop against a wall like that: how muscle works, the smallest particle, the origin of anything. Why color is pleasurable; what pleasure is.

I sit again at the top of the field, with the October sun in my face, looking out over meadow grass and dying wildflowers. Amusing myself once more by flipping the focus of my eyes from visual plane to visual plane, looking at backlit maple leaves and blades of grass, tumbling insects, highlights flickering off and on from shiny leaves on distant bushes. Then on past all that into the cavern of shaded hemlock woods at the edge of the field, up the ridgeline, off into true blue space complete with contrails. And back again: flipping the physiological focus (operating muscles to change the thickness of the lens of my eyeballs), flipping my attention with my focus, keeping it out there, out there. Flipping my consciousness back and forth across the field like a man flipping cards at a hat. Getting banged around by my senses as I do.

If I turn up missing one of these fine fall days, I joke to Chris, she should look for me lying unconscious in the woods, fevered optic nerves shut down until it gets dark. A family cat, dozing on a windowsill in full sun, struggles comically to get its eyes open wide enough to catch the buzzing fly. I feel the struggle in my own eyes. I have a recurring dream about a light so bright that I can't open my eyes against it. It is different in degree but not in kind, I think, from the light out here now, in the October woods.

All this color is headed, soon enough, for the forest floor, to disappear beneath white snow. (They don't call it fall for nothing.) In April, when the snow has gone again, the newly re-exposed leaf carpet will be a uniform soft, reddish brown, the "riotous" colors of the fall reduced almost to monochrome. No red leaves, no yellow ones (where do those colors go?)—although the uniformity does shade off toward a pointilist yellow under the beeches, back to brown under the oaks. A trained eye could probably identify the species by the color change in the mulch beneath the tree. Mine is not yet trained.

The loop ends in sunken old road with partially cannibalized stone walls on both sides, depressed into a U-shape like a glacial valley, like a giant eaves trough. When the road is backlit just right, you're walking down a warm brown tube all the way back to the house. In between all this russet and umber and burnt sienna there are also stretches where the path is scraped clear and the dark-chocolate brown soil exposed. Where the earth is wet is the darkest, bitterest chocolate of all, almost but not quite black.

Nothing in the woods that I've seen yet is quite pitch black. Fallen leaves in standing water sometimes turn a slimy gray, all the life washed out of them; certain shades of gray tell you immediately that what you're looking at is utterly dead. It is when the color comes back toward the red end of the spectrum that life comes back into it. I hadn't realized that before. The stones I work with are also basically gray, but they don't have the visual deadness to them that gray implies. (I heard of one professional wall-builder who won't work with rocks that have ever been touched with mortar. Kills the stone, he says.) The gray is shot through with greens, browns, even blues, from lichens and mosses. Or oxidation: I have no idea which parts of this surface coloration are biological and which only chemical. Either is lovely. Here and there in the woods I come across such beautiful rocks, covered with such soft green mosses that they make me want to lay my face against them. I want to bring them down and place them here and there about the yard, just to look at, to walk by and maybe give a pat every once in a while. I'd do it if I could get them without disturbing the moss. If the moss wouldn't die when moved out of the forest shade. It is probably not, technically, moss.

———

I stop to examine a dead tree—probably once a yellow birch, although it's hard to tell with all the fungi on it. It's covered with serried masses of wafery fungoid growths, standing out from the trunk like the feathers on an owl's leg. They even feel a little like feathers, soft but springy to the touch. On one side of the tree they're grayish white, on the other, yellow, woodier-looking. The color seems to come from moss; on the north side there's fungus on the tree and moss on the fungus. God knows what's on the moss.

Behind me I hear turmoil from the dogs, who have picked up some scent and have become wildly excited over an otherwise unremarkable fifteen-foot area centered in the middle of the path. They whuff away at the scent as if to smell it all up, absorb it, sweep the area clean of the smell. They lose it, wander off, come back, scurry in various directions. They come back to me, pause, go back to try it again. What in the world are they getting? (I smell nothing.) There's no sign of anything in the path, no struggle, blood, feathers, scat. What is it? What kind of larger world do they inhabit? (How easy it would be to call this disturbance "extrasensory," and invent a ghost, a specter, to blame it on.)

October in the woods is a forced march into the sensory life; I am armed with, let's see, the capacity to discern shapes, motions, and colors, to perceive smells, hear sounds. I can also touch things, feel their textures, taste them if I dare. But that's about it, in the way of experiencing the woods. Except, that is, for proprioception, self-sensing, without which I couldn't get into the woods to enjoy them. Proprioception is the sense that makes the first five work, that fetches pleasure (and pain and everything else) and brings it home to us. It is seldom mentioned except among physiologists, an almost secret capacity that explains a huge part of how we experience the world.

Surgically deafened songbirds were found to sing their songs as well after the surgery as before. (Science can be hideous.) They sing, we must assume, by how the song feels to sing, rather than by how it sounds. (But then any division of the senses is arbitrary. Auditory clicks produce measurable electrical activity in the optic nerve. Are we seeing these clicks? Is the eye hearing them?) To sing by feel rather than sound is to sing by proprioception. The proprioceptors are nerve endings embedded throughout the muscle, tendons, and joints of the body that read and report on relative position of body parts, on movement, loading, acceleration and deceleration. They make the musculoskeletal system the largest sense organ of the body, a receptor as well as an effector. Proprioceptors are the neural devices that weigh and judge and perceive whatever we do with that muscle, from performing eye surgery to hitting high C to levering a two-hundred-pound stone into place in the footing of a wall. They tell us where we are and what we're doing as we are doing it; they are our connection to the present tense of physical action.

Some of us get very good with our proprioceptors. Those who do are frequently called athletes, or performers. Playing a violin concerto, for example, may be as dazzling a demonstration of proprioceptive capability as man has yet devised. (And oh, by the way, it's hot in the hall tonight, your fingers will have to rewrite the music to fit the sag of the strings as your performance goes along.) Those of us who don't get good at proprioception are called spectators.

––––––

A group of athletes is asked to rehearse the skills of their sport in their minds alone, without actual movement, while wired to electronic sensors. The sensors indicate that the motionless athletes are actually firing the same muscles, in the same sequence and with the same timing, that they would if they were actually performing the sport. That is, the physical act is in the musculature as well as the mind.

When I do manage to listen to the cries of birds, where I feel it is in my throat—in the place where singing would take place, if I could sing. I can't fly either, but when I watch bird flight (as I do more often than I listen to bird song) I feel it in my shoulders. I watch with my shoulders. I'm sure that what is so lovely about bird flight is not simply what the optic nerve sends to the brain, but also what the brain sends to the muscle. The flight of birds is so lovely to me precisely because so much more of my sensory capacity is involved than vision. The guitarist listens to music with his fingers. The fingers may not actually be moving, but that's where the signals are going, are being picked up. I swear it. I've watched musicians listening; I've seen their fingers twitch.

Proprioception is the connective tissue of the sensory system, the sense that orchestrates the other five, that ties them all together into a coherent representation of the world. It is how one walks, sings, lays stones. It enhances the degree of contact of a kiss. How can we think our pleasures come only through the other five?

––––––––

Halloween brings a perfect day, the foliage now mostly gone, a blinding yellow sun throwing long, steel-blue shadows through silhouetted trees. For purposes of walking in the woods, October is the peak of the year, the absolute high point—which is reason enough, as I see it, for postponing stone work and other duties. Besides, the seventy feet of wall that's done is long enough. It fills the space it was supposed to fill. It does need an ending, a piece of design that says that this is where this particular segment comes to an end. It'd be nicer to look at, over the coming winter, if I finished that part before the snow, but I won't. In the spring, maybe. It is not, after all, to keep the cows in.

At the top of the hill, in late afternoon, I wander into an area I don't recall seeing before, and come across a maple stump five feet thick, still standing eight feet high. The tree that it once was seems to have imploded, falling in on itself like one of those dynamited buildings so beloved in the film-clip business. It's partially blackened; it must have been hit by lightning, thirty or forty years ago. Its former limbs, themselves two feet thick, are still piled crazily every which way around the stump; I try to step up onto one of them and sink to my knee in the punky wood, freezing that way—amazed, wondering at the unimaginable organisms burrowing away in there, reducing lignin to fluff, to down. The stump itself is equally rotten, but on one side there's a patch the size of a couple of washtubs where the bark looks absolutely sound, looks as if the tree is still growing. Of course it's been dead for decades, it's only the chitin—the horn of the tree, its fingernail—but it looks just like the stuff you'd see on a perfectly healthy, growing specimen.

Not far from it is a huge snag, a dead maple still standing, intact but absolutely bare, polished: an ex-tree, a monument to a tree-that-was. It sticks up a good twenty feet above the rest of the canopy, a Grand Central Station for birds. ("Leave your snags," a forester told me. "The wildlife love 'em.") It and the rotten stump are in a parklike flat near the crest of the hill. The remaining, living trees are far enough apart that my eyes are continually swept upward to the canopy: there aren't many limbs at all for the first thirty feet. In the process I spot a deadfall, a huge limb that has broken off and then caught, hanging, a thousand-pound trap. It occurs to me that to walk under it at exactly the wrong time, with the wrong breeze, could mean erasure, as simply and cleanly as my boot erases God knows what organisms beneath my feet. As my computer erases files.

We walk around it and on through the woods, the dogs and I, Pawnee's ruff rising and falling again at exotic autumnal scents. I wish again that I had access to their sources of information, but maybe it's just as well I don't: all three of us are a little drunk by now, sensorily, I think. On days like this you don't dare stop and look at these woods hard anyway, not for very long at a time. If you did you'd burst.

Wading on through fallen leaves, I make one more small mental obeisance to proprioception, to the entire sensory universe that gives me a self to take out for walks like this. My head tells me this is true—that the senses are where the self comes from—but it is a touch too psychological, and therefore fuzzy, for my tastes. I'm more comfortable with the harder edges of physiology and physics. Ah, that's it: proprioception is where physics and physiology come together. That must be why it fascinates me so. It's the tool that helps you get the physics right, the means by which you get the pleasure out of physics. It is the internal rigging that locates the body in time and space, the three-dimensional internal map of the body that redraws itself, realigns itself, with every move you make.

I've been thinking and writing about proprioception for ten years now, in one forum or another, and keep failing to get its wonders adequately set down, the impossible riches brought to us in those mysterious moments when information turns into experience. Can't find a way to say it hard enough, can't sing that clear, clean line.

My frustration reminds me of Lewis Thomas's essay "On Embryology," in *The Medusa and the Snail.* He is speaking of the process that at some point switches on a single cell and allows it to grow into the brain. "No one has the ghost of an idea how this works," he says, "and nothing else in life can ever be so puzzling. If anyone does succeed in explaining it, within my lifetime, I will charter a skywriting airplane, maybe a whole fleet of them, and send them aloft to write one great exclamation point after another, around the whole sky, until all my money runs out."

[12]

NOVEMBER:
OLD GUYS

The woods go silver in November, almost transparent—and so, in some faltering, autumnal way, do I. The understory vegetation is gone now, the woods spare, a little gaunt, opened up to reveal the shape of the land. Snow comes and goes over a long succession of gray, thirty-five-degree days; with or without snow the loop stays slick, its trail underlain with sodden leaves, the footing treacherous. There's a weakness to the light, draining the woods of their dramatics. This morning we get a break, a bright sun and a whippy little north wind around the house, but in the woods all is calm. With four inches of crusty snow, the loop is a real slog: I break through and extricate myself again with every step. Halfway around, the dogs and I come across a patch of bloody snow where some predator has scored. Or I come across it; this time it's the dogs who don't pick it up, getting well past—downwind, to the south—before they do a twenty-yard double take and scamper comically back to investigate. I can't even feel a breeze, never mind smelling anything.

Down below, the new deck is almost finished—just in time to be buried under snow for the winter. We'd been trying since last spring to get a deck built on the west side of the house, a nicer one than my skills as a carpenter would allow. For this we hired Ed, the friend of a friend—somewhat nervously, never having seen his work—but a local building boom kept him from getting started until the fall. To reduce the cost, and to learn some carpentry, I volunteered as helper, full-time gofer, holder of the other end of boards. On the first day Ed produced a jackhammer and set me to work demolishing an old concrete stair—a new experience, running a jackhammer, and one that doesn't need repeating. The first few hours at it demonstrated that stone work had not made me as fit for hard labor as I had thought, and by nightfall I was doing some serious rethinking of my volunteer role, worried that I might not be physically able to continue. But over the next few days the aches began to go away, as I trained up for it, just as in athletics. I can still get in shape for work like this, I realized, I just don't want to.

With snow on the ground, work on the wall is out of the question. It's no fun when your hands are cold anyway, and I got enough of that finishing the deck, sticking out into the north wind like the prow of a ship. On many mornings there would be a rim of ice or a few inches of snow on the lumber. Ed would arrive at eight wearing long johns, bundled up in a hooded sweatshirt and down vest. I'd join him, similarly attired but also wearing gloves, which Ed disdained. This wasn't carpenter's machismo, but simple adaptation: he'd worked outdoors well into winter in the past, and would again, and there was no point in losing toughness painfully acquired. I once read of mountain-climbers who, in order to train their hands, skied through a winter without gloves, so I guess it can be done. Not by me.

Mostly what I learned from helping Ed was patience. I may not have acquired it, but at least I learned how necessary it was, how I would somehow have to find it if I were going to get any better at that kind of work. He turned out to be quite a good carpenter, putting my nervousness to rest. Better at some things than others, of course; during the foundation stage I thought I might kill him—just brain him with a handy two-by-four and cover his body with concrete—owing to a certain casualness in matters of grade and dimension. (He had learned his trade on the West Coast.) The deck that grew to fit the foundations we poured was somewhat larger and of a slightly different shape than the deck we'd planned, in part because Ed left the drawings at home that day. But it turned out okay, as he kept assuring me it would. Precision was not as important at that stage as I'd thought. "I'm really a finish guy, anyway," Ed would say about large structural matters.

He was indeed, and with the foundation in and the framework laid out, he put together a beautiful deck, with loving attention to detail. He did it approximately on budget, out of frightfully expensive redwood, and when it was finished I found only a couple of pieces of leftover scrap more than two feet long. What's more, he did it with me looking over his shoulder at every saw cut, and he didn't brain me, which may have been the most artistic accomplishment of all.

———

Watching closely while someone else works is remarkably misleading. It's almost as if the different viewpoint reveals different physics; what looks like it goes real easy goes less so the moment the tool is in your own hand. To speed the work, I would try to have the next board handy, or otherwise predict the obvious next move. My prediction was usually wrong; Ed, seeing the task close up and having a clearer order of procedure in mind, would veer off in some other direction. Thus he kept me off-balance. He seemed accustomed, though, to working with a totally ignorant assistant, explaining easily and clearly what I should do next and why. Thus he kept me on track.

This chatty style of work was foreign to me, and it took a few days for us to agree on a common language, a way of describing carpentry details that I could understand—perhaps because of my background in the grunt-and-point school. I'm generally incapable of that kind of explanation myself: when it's someone helping me, I don't know how to describe what needs to be done next. I'd always assumed my stepfather worked that way out of sullen disdain, but I now realize it could also have been because he didn't have the language for it either. He didn't say much about anything, ever. Of course it could also have arisen from a certain diffidence—an embarrassment at pointing out what should be obvious to anyone with a lick of sense. Could I have been misinterpreting my stepfather's motives for all these years? Nah.

Ed and I talked from time to time about craftsmanship, and other aspects of work that might be called ideational, but only on a purely practical level. He subscribed to various esoteric trade journals, and would show me articles by the more thoughtful practitioners. "Some of these guys really get into process," he said. "They talk about it a lot. Like, 'It isn't the product that counts, but just doing it, you know? The *process.*'" It is a sentiment for which we both expressed some sympathy, but Ed pointed out that the process guys don't get, you know, hired much: too few clients willing to pay a guy for enjoying himself.

Carpentry also suffers, like other arts, from an insufficiency of patrons.

Building the deck was real work all right, hammers and saws, all day every day, answering to Ed's schedule rather than my own. Just like a job. Demonstrating more eloquently than stone work had ever done what a dilettantish thing I was doing when I played around with my wall. What it required physically was pure stamina, to deal with the ongoing fatigue. By midafternoon in the November cold I'd be stumbling, no longer trusting myself to attempt anything that required more than the most fumbling efforts. Ed would go right on doing delicate or difficult work, maintaining a fine balance between the urge to get the job done and the patience to do it right. I couldn't maintain that balance and didn't really try. Didn't have to. Ed's helper, who wasn't much of a carpenter to start with, got steadily worse—stupider, and less ambitious—as the day wore on.

The weather finally got too damned cold for me, and I packed it in. All that remained was the very fine finish work anyway, which required a very fine patience (and none of my ham-handed skills), and I was pretty much reduced to standing around shivering while Ed fitted very fine wood into very fine joints. While I twitched nervously, brooding about the cost of the lumber, the cost of his time, the non-income-generating cost of my own. So I abandoned it to him—to his great relief, I'm sure—and came indoors. There were still a couple of chores that had to be done to get the place ready for winter, but otherwise, I decided, it was time for the great out-of-doors to start coming in shorter doses.

Ed's patience, especially in the cold, never stopped amazing me. It made me think that I should have gone ahead and built a stone wall at my usual slapdash pace, then used that wall as a stockpile of stones from which to build the real one, carefully fitted, next to it. Which suddenly gave me the image of an endless succession of walls marching sideways down the hillside, each slightly neater than the last.

Carpentry in the real world, I learned, is to an alarming extent a process of scattering a huge supply of building materials and an enormous number of tools all around the work site, and then fetching what you need next from that assortment: kneeling down and getting up again, climbing over various barriers and up and down ladders, crawling under things, remembering too late which tools and nails you're going to need to do what it was that got you into that awkward position in the first place, working at the limits of your reach. It may be that more patience is required for the gathering of the right materials and tools in the place where you can apply them to each other than for the careful fitting of joints. To have a gofer, therefore, is efficient—if he knows the names of things, and can remember where you left them last time you used them.

When I do projects of my own, the problem is not so much with patience as with attention. As long as I keep patience in mind—lecturing myself about slowing down, easing up, taking a little off the effort—I'm fine. To do the job, however, eventually requires thinking about the work itself, and when I do that, I start going at it too hard, too fast. Killing snakes.

As a kid, circumstances convinced me that work had to be a struggle, invested with something very like anger. God knows I've done enough projects that way to last a lifetime: that particular mental set is still hanging right there in the closet, ready as a war bonnet. I used to break tools. Ott, in charge of both the tools and the tasks on which I was to use them, accused me of breaking them to get out of the work. When I splintered one of the wooden handles on the post-hole digger, he replaced both handles with welded steel pipe, adding another thirty pounds to the weight that had to be lifted and slammed, over and over again, into our rock-hard caliche "soil" to dig post-holes. Making the handles out of heavy pipe was vengeful, I thought, which was also the spirit in which I'd been wielding them before they broke, and in which I wielded them ever after. I wasn't crafty enough to break them to avoid work; I broke them by whacking at things too hard with them, equally angry at the things, the tools, the task itself. I started investing work with an emotional load about the time of my first household chore. I don't know why.

I would like to believe that that anger has been considerably eased by now, but there have been times when stone work turned ugly on me, when control began to slip away. If the bugs were bad and the humidity high, if I tried to fit a session of stone work into too tight a day, the old habits returned. The wall, the stones, gravity itself, became oppressors. I would begin wanting too much—from the available time, from myself, from those dumb objects—and start killing snakes again.

Maybe I should learn to whistle, or hum along under my breath. Just once I'd like to come to the end of some task like washing the dishes without my forehead wrinkled into a grimace and my shoulders screwed up around my ears. Straining against nothing but myself. I start around the loop on a frigid morning and notice that Molly, the older dog, is not moving very well, a little tentative. She does a bad job of leaping the brook, and then I, following, do a bad job of it too. I'm walking all hunched up, unsure, tense; if I'd just relax and straighten up, I could move with a great deal more assurance and flow, more enjoyment. Stop walking like an old man, I say to myself, and do

so—for ten paces, maybe, and then I'm thinking about something else and my shoulders are firmly attached to my ears
again. I wish I could just change.

Deciding to change is a little like deciding to be smart: not
a decision I can make. I have not found a way to teach myself
to be the other thing, the thing I want to change into. It needs
something like athletic training, causing change to occur at
the level of muscle fiber, connective tissue, nerve ending. I'm
not sure this is a metaphor. Which are the nerve endings that
make me reach for the button in the elevator, the one marked
"close"?

I bailed out of the deck project early in November and, knowing
that at any moment winter would clang shut the door, set about
battening down the place: putting the tractor up on blocks,
hauling in lawn and garden stuff, winding hoses and draining
faucets while the dark wind blew, getting the storm windows
on and sealed. Bolting down hatches, reefing sails.

The shorter November's days become, in their shocking
plunge into winter, the more obsessive I am about getting
around the loop. Even while I was working with Ed, I'd wait
for the moment he went home for lunch, then be off like a
shot. After I quit and came inside, I'd work at my desk until
I heard his truck leave, then bolt for the door—not having the
chutzpah to stroll off into the woods while he was there doing
honest labor.

I don't know why, but there's more carrion around in the
late fall. Maybe the onset of cold weather kills off creatures
too weak to make it through the winter, leaving them to rot
instead of being sanitarily eaten by predators. (Willy suggests
that the scavengers may have gone south, or into hibernation.)
Anyway, it attracts the dogs. They stay with me on the trail

only until they smell something interesting, which they then go find. Usually it is not carrion, and they smell it carefully and then return. If it is carrion, they roll in it first, decorating their withers, and come back prancing with joy and self-importance, trying to decorate me, too.

If I'm paying attention I can call them back before they get into the noisome stuff, but my mind wanders. Earlier this month Pawnee returned from one of these side trips with the silly grin that indicated she had a small treasure in her mouth—one that Molly or I should try to steal. It was the skull of some small mammal, a weasel or something, with enough flesh left on it to stink horribly. I got it away from her and put it well up out of reach in the crotch of a tree (breaking her heart and Molly's too, and ensuring a pilgrimage to that particular spot on every walk for the next several years). In the process I had to handle skull and dog, and by the time we got back to the house we both urgently needed a bath. I left parka and gloves outdoors, took Pawnee directly to the basement and bathed her, stripped and threw my clothes into the laundry, and took a shower myself.

It didn't really help, not enough. The smell—that awful, psychically terrorizing smell of death—kept hanging around for the rest of the day, in spite of anything I could do. It's been giving me the creeps ever since, that charnel-house aspect of death. I can't imagine why dogs are so attracted to it. The experts' explanations for this behavior are unsatisfactory. It makes me consider not taking the dogs with me into the woods for a while, at least until everything is covered by a sufficiently protective layer of snow.

Then, a day or two before my upcoming fifty-fifth birthday, one of our two old cats had a stroke, and began listing around the house, crashing into walls, unable to stand. These were *very* old cats, a mother and daughter. (The mother was born the summer of Robert Kennedy's assassination.) It was the daughter that had the stroke, and we knew immediately that she would have to be put down. The mother was already deaf, mostly blind, incontinent, had been for some time. The two were inseparable. It would be crueler, we realized, to leave the old mother alone than to go ahead and put her, too, out of her misery.

So on the morning of my birthday, we took them to the vet's and had the deed mercifully, quickly done, and brought the pathetic old bodies home, where, in a cold, sleety rain, I buried them. Deep. That, I announced, was the absolute guaranteed last goddamned outdoor chore of the year. Another couple of weeks and the ground would have been frozen and we couldn't have done it anyway. Those two old cats had been damned nuisances for years, and we eased them out of our lives (and theirs) with a sigh of relief. Matter-of-factly decided, matter-of-factly done. Except that we could barely speak to each other for about ten days, and would wait a whole two weeks after that before we got a new kitten.

The evening after the disposition of the cats, Willy came over—Liz was out of town—for a determinedly noncelebratory birthday dinner. We never mentioned the cats, or much of anything else, I'm afraid. Weird evening: he must have wondered what the hell was going on. Late fall may not be the best time of year for the dispatch of elderly animals.

———

My birthday joke this year was that having attained the great age of fifty-five, I would retire. Sit around the house and, I don't know, write books or something. It was a thin joke at best, which nobody but me seemed to think was funny.

For my fiftieth birthday—the last previous one to which I'd

given much conscious thought—the joke had been that I wouldn't have it. Chris had suggested a gathering of friends, but I said no thanks, I had other fish to fry. I was being an athlete in those days, and celebrated by (over)training myself into a sodden lump. There's a perfectly nice theory that physical training reduces, or perhaps even reverses, aging. Aging is a disease of too little movement, of hypokinesis; hyper*kinesis* should be its antidote. So my fiftieth birthday present to myself was a spate of particularly heavy training. Went at it like killing you-know-whats, ended up killing muscles and joints instead.

For my fifty-fifth birthday, the joke was rather the opposite, having to do with getting off my own back. What made the retirement business a joke—to me, anyway—was that it would permit me somehow to reduce the urgency that informed my customary approach to things. That I had been trying, and failing, to reduce for the previous twenty years. The difference was that I'd never attached the word "retirement" to this effort before. The word was somehow going to make it happen. No wonder nobody thought this was funny.

Perhaps all I'm talking about here is Type A versus Type B behavior. I have a file on that. Type A individuals are the driven ones, who, in some studies, seem to run a high risk of heart attack. They've had some success lowering the risk with behavior modification techniques: driving in the slow lane on freeways, choosing the longest line at the supermarket checkout, and other rituals. My most recent behavioral modification technique has been stone work, which sometimes worked, a little. I'll have to come up with some others. I can do this. I am full of plans for a life of mindfulness, which I intend to start pursuing any day now.

———

A certain personal gloominess seems to set in in November anyway, starting, probably, when we go off daylight saving time at the end of October and lose one more hour out of days already grown depressingly short. I chose this period to haul an assortment of physical complaints off to the medical profession and was finally convinced, by experts, that what I thought was chronic tendinitis was in fact a mild, not particularly common form of arthritis. Not a tragedy, just a nuisance. Depressing. This is not the first time I've become depressed in the late fall. For a long time I regarded it as nothing more than an annual phobic reaction to the onset of the Christmas season—my fear of ceremony being surpassed only by an inborn panic at the threat of group activities.

I found reassurance, then, when the media began running their annual assortment of pop-science pieces about Seasonal Affective Disorder, or SAD. That's the trendy new scientific name for autumnal blues: an actual hormonal disturbance resulting from the shortening of the days. They've been talking about it for a few years now; medical science has finally come up with a disease for those of us who regularly find November more difficult than October, and December more difficult than November. We can begin to breathe a sigh of relief: thank God, it's real, it's hormones and not madness. *It's not our fault,* we shriek; they've finally jacked up our craziness and run a little physiology under it. (Are *you* willing to accept responsibility for your behavior, to vouch for its rationality from, say, November 15 to February 15 of last year? Think about it.)

My personal version of this affliction is also mild; full-blown cases suffer loss of sleep, appetite, and libido, generalized depression, and other gruesome symptoms. I only get . . . sad. The thing is, I think everyone else does too. I am personally convinced that there are as many degrees or levels of SAD as there are people, although science hasn't pronounced on this yet. We borderline cases just go a little bit crazy: mood swings, fits of anger, gloom. Carbohydrate cravings, yes, lots of *soft* foods. In November, the dishwasher fills up with spoons and bowls. The professional trend-spotters call this last part of the behavior "cocooning." I'm not sure they've noticed how closely it is tied to the season.

SAD is a wonderful excuse: it isn't the shorter days and longer nights, or being forced to come indoors, or the uniformly lousy weather, or the frantic work schedules to clear holiday vacation time, or the necessity of travel at the most crowded and dangerous time of the year, or the greed of the merchants and the guilt associated with the gift racket, or the impending hysterical holiday rituals and the emotional extortion they always generate—or the tinsel falseness of our pathetic attempts to decorate our world against the dying of the light—that makes us blue in the fall. It's just hormones. Some of us need to hibernate. Some of us need to damp down our metabolism in a dark hole somewhere, and be left alone to gloom our way through until the sun begins to come back. Others of us don't. Some of us get knocked far enough off balance that we go medical, and the scientific mind can finally get a grasp on what the problem is. Most of us aren't that bad off, we're just gloomy. I'm not sure whether Seasonal Affective Disorder is a disease or a belief system, but no matter. I think it nice of science to come up with a physical explanation, right there in the biochemistry, to let us SADists off this hook.

––––––––

November grinds darkly on, and the snow begins to get serious. I slog through it for as long as I can, but eventually it gets either too deep or too icy. When depth is the problem I can switch to skis or snowshoes, but this year, as often happens, we get freezing rain on top of snow, setting up such a glaze that skis or snowshoes can get no purchase. Ice skates would be more in order; to walk in ordinary boots is to ask for fractures. (Last year in these conditions I put on my skis at the back door, pushed off, fell instantly, and slid on my back the seventy-five yards down to the pond before I could stop. Had to take my skis off and virtually crawl back up to the house.) What I need are mountaineer's crampons.

I am determined not to give up the loop, not even long enough to wait for the next, softening snowfall. I am also determined, in some peculiarly crotchety way that I don't quite understand, not to buy a real set of crampons: too expensive, too formalized somehow, even if I knew where to get them. I decide instead to invent my own. I dig out an old pair of rubbers and push a handful of thumbtacks through the soles of each, from the inside out. I slip the rubbers over hiking boots, and set out. Perfect: like you've just stepped out of the rosin box, like gum-rubber soles on a freshly varnished gym floor. Very comfortable, stable, safe, you don't know you've got them on. I'm a genius.

Except that I gradually lose that reassuring traction, and when I finish the loop and take the rubbers off, the heads of the thumbtacks pour out in my hand. Friction has broken off all the points. I need a heavier grade of tack. Nothing in the garage or the basement fits the bill, so I drive into town, to the hardware store. I browse the racks of brads and fasteners, considering carpet tacks versus upholstery tacks, roofing tacks, brads, big-headed nails, certain that just the right tack exists for my purposes, a vision of the perfect solution in my head. A salesperson offers assistance, but I am loath even to attempt an explanation of the peculiar specificity of my needs, and wave her off. Trying to get the physics right, I notice, can lead to a certain fussiness.

It is three-thirty on a gray November afternoon, the hardware store somnolent under flickering fluorescence. The quietness penetrates my attention, and I look around. It's a large, modern store, and scattered here and there along the aisles are five or six old guys, picking through the racks of stuff. Must drive the sales force crazy, I think to myself, as my fingers flutter over the packages of tacks.

I describe this scene to Chris. "Right," she says. "Old guys: more and more intelligence focused on smaller and smaller problems."

Not intelligence—wisdom, says I. We old guys have much wisdom to offer on subjects such as tacks.

WINTER

PART IV

[13]

SOLSTICE:
THE ANXIOUS
FOOL

The tilting of the earth may very well have stopped at the winter
solstice, creaking to a halt and starting back the other way,
but I was down in the basement at the time, running a power
saw, and didn't feel a thing. I was busy building the last of
the bluebird houses for this year's Christmas presents.

When we moved to this house, a neighbor, Mr. Mott,
dropped by and presented us with four bluebird houses. We
set them out, and have had bluebirds every summer since.
This October one of the houses blew down, and was too rotten
to repair. I made a new one out of redwood scrap I'd saved
from the deck, using the pieces of the old birdhouse as a
pattern. This mini-carpentry started me thinking what a nice
gift the birdhouses had been when we moved in, what a lift it
was every spring when the bluebirds came back. This was the
gift-giving season; why not pass along the favor? So in December, as we approached the solstice, I got busy building birdhouses. There was a fine ceremonial resonance to it, I have to

167

admit, building next spring's bluebird houses as we plunged deeper down the dark hole of winter. More resonance for me, perhaps, than for anyone I'd be giving them to. With the old birdhouse as pattern, I didn't have to be much of a carpenter, although that doesn't mean I got the wood sizes and nails right. I ran into Mott at the post office and mentioned that my carpentry wasn't up to his standard. That's okay, he said, the rougher the carpentry, the better the bluebirds seem to like the house. Another nice gift.

Tree swallows also like the houses, and bluebirds are stubbornly territorial, so every spring there's a lot of aerial mock-combat over who gets which houses. That's okay too; they work it out, and the swirling bird life is a continual pleasure, for us and for the birds too, I think. Our place is on a dead-end road and was unoccupied for a couple of years before we moved in. At first there was a disturbing lack of bird life, even when we put out feeders. After a few weeks of our coming and going, though—of life in the house again—the birds came back. They like action, I believe, just the way dogs love to mill.

Coming indoors for the season is always considerably encouraged by the first big storm of the winter, and this year was no exception. We got eight or ten inches of fluffy powder out of a quiet, warm, decidedly unstormy storm. I went out in it like a little kid, skiing the loop at the height of the snowfall, watching the woods grow peaceful, thinking about angels.

This storm, like all our big ones, arrived courtesy of an east wind, although the air was dead calm by the time the snow fell. If the wind gets the slightest bit east of due north or due south, it has a dubious feel to it, telling us that something wet is going to happen. (We get storms from the north and west, too, but not as dramatic.) The local prevailing wind is from

the west, indicating only more of the same, so we hardly notice
it. When it swings around to the north it becomes bracing, of
course, sweeping out the haze. (Sometimes in the winter, "bracing" doesn't say it by half: it can settle into the north for days
at a time, howling and shaking the house, setting our nerves
on edge, plunging the thermometer lower every night. The dogs
and cats get edgy too.) When the wind is from the south it
stinks, carrying atmospheric crap up from the coastal mega-
lopolis, swelling my nasal passages, making me feel mean.
Maybe what comes riding on the wind from that direction is
memories.

I didn't know we knew any of this until Chris came in from
throwing the Frisbees for the dogs one evening and predicted
rain. East wind. Frisbees make you notice the direction of the
wind, because that determines which side of the house you
throw from. Since one of us throws them every day, we always
know the wind direction—but for purposes of dog exercise,
not necessarily for weather prediction. Now that I've begun
thinking about it, I believe I might be able to tell the wind
direction from the smell alone, although I can't describe the
smells. (Pause to consider testing this skill scientifically: a
blindfold, Chris leading me outdoors, et cetera. Too much trouble. I didn't make this claim as a bar bet.) In the city I always
knew where north was, but I hadn't a clue—literally as well
as figuratively—to which way the wind was blowing. It blows
in different directions there, from block to block.

I still haven't learned to think of east as "east," but just as
over there, the direction the rain comes from. Moss actually
does grow on the north side of trees, the shadiest side. In the
woods I usually know without thinking which side of the tree
is likely to have moss on it, although if I carry a compass, I
am often shocked at where the needle wants to point. Maybe

the moss could unbox my interior compass: all I'd have to do is stop being concerned about what's labeled north and pay more attention to which way is most hidden from the sun.

For the last few years one of our Christmas rituals has been an annual concert by the Boston Camerata, one of those organizations devoted to the preservation and performance of medieval music. Chris and I both love the traditional Christmas music, and have it playing in the house during the holidays. When we heard the Camerata would give a local concert, it sounded like a wonderful supplement to our holiday music, so we bought tickets.

It didn't turn out quite the way I'd pictured it. The group's approach is scholarly, presenting very old, very foreign music on medieval instruments (the shawm, the rebec, the sackbut). Very little of the music is even remotely familiar, and the scholarship behind it is wasted on musically illiterate me. At my impoverished level of appreciation, it is frankly pretty boring, and if the concert weren't given in an old church with excruciatingly uncomfortable vertical-backed pews, I'd have even more trouble staying awake. Chris really enjoys it, but I don't know why I keep going back.

Except that when I think about Christmas now, that bleating, honking music, sung in unintelligible tongues, keeps coming back to mind. It somehow drives Christmas back through the centuries for me, stripping it clean. The words are all about Jesus, but what the music is about feels far older than Christ. It is whistling against the solstician dark, I think, attempted magic—and a more human response to the black end of the year than stuffy religiosity ordinarily allows. Not a bit comforting, and so it helps jar me out of my Christmas torpor. I guess I'll suffer through it again this year—although penance is another one of those traditions I'd prefer not to believe in.

When my first child was born, I dropped out of school to pay some bills. For a while I worked as a lab assistant in a research institute on the campus of a fine old liberal arts college. Each year the male members of the freshman class served as experimental subjects for our lab, thanks to the president of the college, who volunteered them. (Arrogances of that stripe were routine in 1953.) The experiment was a nasty one, involving harmless but unpleasant electric shocks administered at unpredictable intervals. The scientist who designed it felt we needed some predictor to tell us which subjects might have problems getting through the session. So a test was inserted, among the various other forms that the incoming freshmen filled out, that was designed to measure the individual's level of anxiety.

We never saw the test, only the numerical scores for the arriving subjects. We were told to expect problems when the anxiety index was twenty or above. If a subject simply refused, there was nothing to do but let him go, but we were expected to cajole him along as far as possible. We didn't lose many. One we did lose had an anxiety index of forty-one. He was a bright, engaging, even cheerful guy, but he unvolunteered himself before we got him inside the door of the lab, never mind about hooking up any wires.

We also tested a subject whose anxiety index was three. We would see the scores the day before a subject came in, and this one prompted a lot of jokes. He'd probably be delivered in a wheelbarrow, we said, a 160-pound cabbage. I was fascinated by the very idea that someone might be so comfortable in his own skin, and when he arrived I struck up a conversation, trying to get a sense of the person.

He was a wiry, red-headed Korean War vet, a dozen years older than the usual freshman, quite a bit older than me, too. He was late entering college not only because of military service but because he'd homesteaded in Canada for several years. He'd gone off into the bush, staked out land and built a cabin, and lived there for a while as a subsistence farmer. Oh God, I said, I *love* Thoreau, I wanted to *memorize* Walden. How was it, what was that like? "Well," he said, "just about like anything else. You can worry about the Internal Revenue Service, or you can worry about where you're going to get some more beans for your plate. If you're going to worry, it doesn't make much difference which."

Right, of course, that's it, I told myself at the time, that's the answer. I swore to myself then and there—at about age twenty—that that was the attitude I would take. I, too, would have a low anxiety index. A few years later a friend of mine lost most of his stomach to ulcers; watching him drink milk and take small bites of soda crackers, I kept wondering why he didn't just relax, cool out, stop consuming himself that way. Not me, boy, *I* would never be anxious. Within another few years I was having similar symptoms. I was working in advertising and my marriage was breaking up, and I knew for certain that if I didn't yet have an ulcer, one was certainly on the way.

A doctor put me through the barium breakfast routine, and as I waited for the results, I promised myself that as soon as the ulcer was diagnosed, that was it, I was really going to relax, take the pressure off myself, lower my anxiety index. I didn't for a moment consider changing my obviously poisonous life; I assumed that the message itself—the establishment of the fact of an ulcer—would do the changing for me. In a way, it did: when they told me I didn't have an ulcer after all, the symptoms cleared up and have never returned. I've never discovered where I put them after I took them out of my gut.

I don't know whatever happened to Mr. Anxiety Index Three, but by curious circumstance I have been able to keep track of the fellow with the score of forty-one. He became a writer.

If you know the difference between bells at Christmas and trumpets at Easter, you're ready for heaven, a college professor of mine said once. Knowing nothing about religions, I doubt I got the point, but it had such a neat rhetorical flourish to it that I've never forgotten the remark. I would prefer not to bring religions into this discussion. It is embarrassing enough putting my idiotic gloom up against sugarplums and shiny new toys, never mind babes in mangers. I love and enjoy my family, want to love and enjoy all family occasions, and most of the time I do, but I have overcome long odds to do so. The family Christmas gatherings I grew up with were mostly the occasions of quarreling among drunken adults, at least as I remember them. My own children's associations may well be similar, except that the adults were perhaps a little less drunk—and totally unquarrelsome, opting instead for silence (hostile or otherwise). I don't mean to be cynical about this, quite the opposite. I'm all for it, the whole show, days and nights of fond indulgence, the groaning board and rich red wine, glorious voices singing of the purest babe. I *want* Christmas, want to open up to it, unlock, accept it all. But I am frozen on the edge. I still don't know how, after fifty-five of them, to handle it.

As the season draws nearer, certain holiday responsibilities loom, but I find myself unable to think about them, about

Christmas in any form. My mind shuts down, refusing the subject. I get great pleasure thinking about the Jesus story, love it that we have this holy birth to symbolize the turn of the year, but I can't put Christ back into Christmas any better than anyone else. It is the marketing of festivity, I think, that is behind my despair. It sends me back down to build more birdhouses. I'm rather taken with the image of myself as the genial old guy puttering around in the basement, tap-tap-tacking together gifts for loved ones, but it isn't exactly accurate. It is really more of an old guy in a gloomy rage, slamming birdhouses together any way he can, get the goddamned things out of here, get back upstairs and pour himself a hooker of gin, turn on the TV. Hunker down until this mess is over with. They're terrible birdhouses, crappy little birdhouses, an embarrassment of a gift. Why do I get myself into these things?

Religion would surely help, I'm sure of that, if I had some. I seem to have been successfully inoculated against it in elementary school, along with smallpox and the other childhood diseases. My mother was a lukewarm Protestant (but the firmest of believers), my father a scornful atheist, my stepfather noncommittal—although Ott did seem to try to soften a bit, a few years before his death. I was sent to local fundamentalist Sunday schools, but soon rebelled at that. I still believed, in furious resistance to my father's sarcastic atheism, until about puberty. Then one day my friend David announced that he didn't believe in God, and I immediately said, Oh, I don't either, and felt a clear ray of freedom touch my mind: of course, of course, I didn't have to believe all that stuff. Chris describes a similar moment, when she first discovered the possibility of unvocalized thought. You could just think things, anything you wanted to, and you didn't have to tell. The world opened up with heady new possibilities.

The next fall my father died. I steel-eyed my way through the funeral, already hurt enough by his drinking to have written him off. I can remember making that conscious decision when I got the news: his death was to be a relief. At Ott's funeral—I was in my forties by then—I was positively giddy, if for no other reason than that I was now able to visit my mother without his brooding presence. When she in turn died, a decade later, she had been grotesquely ill with lung cancer for several months, confined to a nursing home with no prospect of recovery. Her death was such a relief that it left me sincerely thankful, which I suppose started me thinking: to what?

Anyone else's stone wall is an obvious, and rather pathetic, attempt at monument-building, but I don't do corny crap like that.

Writing off the two male parents in my life before they died was a damned handy device. Funny how I never noticed that it writes me off too. It is perhaps time for me to stop waffling and get down to it, after all these dodges. Time to cut bait, mortality-wise. I have figured out a few things about this. It is surely what's behind all this physiology, all the athletic stuff, in my mind. (How ingeniously I've been denying it.) Also mechanics, and physics, science in general, and mathematics, oh definitely mathematics, although I can't say I've made any headway there. All of these ingeniously logical, systematized procedures we go through in pursuit of certitude. Surely my endless talk about a sensory life springs from dread; that must also be the source of the power that physiology has had for me, my tool for understanding the world. Physiology as monkey wrench. Or as comforter, maybe: reducing death to the failure of the cells, a mere loss of the fire. So one more (final) cell winks out, begins its transmutation back into the elements (physiology again giving way to physics): so what? Leave it all to physics, let it all turn back to physics in the end—that glorious science that couldn't light the fire in the cell with two matches and a can of gasoline.

I think I am so fond of the physics of things because it makes me think I am not The Anxious Fool—the creature who sits at the computer, cringes at Christmas, pours the gin. I've never figured out why I can't get rid of him just by changing my mind. I still think I can kill him off by paying better attention. If I can just find something else to pay attention to.

———

Snow falling in the woods when there's no wind is the most peaceful thing I've ever seen. I've tried to figure out why. In a snowstorm the flakes nearest the eye seem to be falling fastest; the farther away, the slower they look to be falling. In a given amount of time, the percentage of your field of vision traversed by the close-up flakes is much greater than is traversed by the flakes that are farther away. This gives a deep dimensionality to your view, rank-ordering the flakes, as you look out through them, in order of decreasing speed. Thus space creates time, in a sense, and time creates space. At infinity, the flakes are stopped dead in their tracks (and inside your skull, the speed of light!). The encyclopedias of my childhood used images like this to explain the theory of relativity. Mr. Frost (watching the woods fill up with snow), meet Mr. Einstein.

Now when snow starts falling, I try to have the good sense to head out into the woods. I discovered this pleasure by accident, in this winter's first big storm. I was shuffling along on skis, thinking I was out there mostly for the exercise, and stopped to look for a moment. The size of the flakes made them fall slowly, softly, no damage done, the world getting its moisture via a pile of feathers. "Peaceful storm" is an oxymoron, which may be why it transfixed me so. There was no ache in

me as I watched it, no ache at all, a subjective state so novel
that it was positively startling. Another of my fantasies is to
carry around in my head a videotape of that snowfall in the
woods, and, when the scurrying starts again, to punch it up
and watch for a bit. A better button, I figure, than the one that
closes, or doesn't close, the elevator doors.

I stood on my skis and watched the snow fall for ten minutes
or so without really knowing I was doing it, the flakes piling
up on my hat, the shoulders of my parka, the backs of my
gloves. That's when I ended up thinking about angels—to my
total surprise, as I couldn't remember ever thinking about
angels before. I was charmed by the very idea. Only one of a
slew of nice ideas, this time of year, if you can cut through to
them. Well, I thought—determined to keep it jokey, even with
my private self—if there is a God, He's out here hiding in the
woods, hiding in the snowstorm, this snowstorm He made to
hide Himself from me. Leaving me worshipping the snowstorm
instead of the God that made it. That's okay too: any port, as
they say, in a storm. The real joke, I guess, has to do with all
those years I was too smart to believe, and now, when I need
it, I'm not smart enough to figure out how. I'll work on it,
though. That, frankly, is what the woods are for.

[14]

WINTER:
JASON'S
SHIELD

Winter darkness brings on the extreme winter depression the Polar Eskimo
call perlerorneq. *According to the anthropologist Jean Malaurie, the*
word means to feel "the weight of life." To look ahead to all that must
be accomplished and to retreat to the present feeling defeated, weary
before starting, a core of anger, a miserable sadness. It is to be "sick of
life" a man named Imina told Malaurie. The victim tears fitfully at his
clothing. A woman begins aimlessly slashing at things in the iglu with
her knife. A person runs half naked into the bitter freezing night, scream-
ing out at the village, eating the shit of the dogs. Eventually the person
is calmed by others in the family, with great compassion, and helped to
sleep. Perlerorneq. *Winter.*

—Barry Lopez, *Arctic Dreams*

Carefully, carefully, now: it might just be possible to make it
through this winter after all. Carefully for the usual reasons of
seasonal looniness, but carefully also because it is a physically
dangerous time, for all our climatological sophistication.
Storms come in series now, each one slamming us around for

a day or two, hammering snow methodically into the minutest cracks, leaving in its wake a hair-raising cold snap. On the long nights when the wind howls, we listen also to the groans of the house, its mechanical systems grinding away at sustaining our lives. The woods are silent, black and white, the wall invisible, a long loaf of snow. A cursory and inconsequential sun barely makes it over the rim of the hill. The air hurts. We lie doggo. Keep still, be patient, take an even strain.

And enjoy the storms. One started at midnight last night, put down a foot of snow by nine in the morning—or put it sideways, rather, building drifts, plastering more of it to vertical surfaces than to horizontal ones—and is still coming down hard. Six above zero, a twenty-mile-per-hour wind; I drink coffee and wait for the plow, a ritual that might be considered the New England regional winter sport. If the plow comes soon, I go for the mail; if not, I . . . wait some more. I wait also for the wind to drop, hoping it will moderate sufficiently to make the loop survivable. It is magnificent in the woods after a big snowfall, but hard to get to, hard to get out of.

When the snow is old and packed, boots or crampons will do, but on new snow, skis—the most awkward sports equipment ever devised—have been the vehicle of choice since I moved to snow country. This winter, though, a guest happened to say that she hated cross-country skiing, and I realized with a jolt of gratitude that I do too. Skiing is a skill, and our wildly varying snow conditions don't allow enough practice to stay sharp. When I'm rusty, which is most of the time, that slick ease with which skis move over the snow turns frightening, and I feel precarious, too many limbs at risk. Skis generate far more adrenaline than I now have any use for. Besides, if you're not doing it for the thrills, skiing serves mostly to reduce the time in the woods, which is the opposite of what I want.

This winter, snowshoes are sparing me all that unbidden adrenaline. They allow perfectly satisfactory access to the woods when the surface is too soft for walking, and are even better exercise than skiing, at least for my tastes. Someone left a pair in the barn years ago, real antiques, five-foot-long monsters. I'd only tried to use them once or twice, back when I was a practiced skier, and found them impossibly clumsy. But the crampons, allowing me to stroll blithely across the ice, had become such a liberating new development that the prospect of returning to skis for deep snow was depressing. So I started learning to use snowshoes.

They're alleged to be next to impossible on hills, and to make you walk straddle-legged, putting an uncomfortable strain on the crotch. Neither is exactly true. I did feel unsteady on them until I thought to take along ski poles, but with that extra outrigging, they're so easy to use that I virtually forget I have them on. And they go—methodically, pedestrianly—anywhere.

Where they go is purely beautiful: in the woods in winter, a good coating of snow hides the minor understory vegetation, so the shape of the terrain comes up more clearly. The white background lays an even texture over every declivity, turning the woods into a collection of soft, voluptuous curves—made hard-edged here and there by old stone walls peeping through the snow. Snowshoes allow me to ignore trails and roam those curves. The snow's clean plasticity cosmetizes everything, hiding all that messy fertility; I tramp across it enjoying the thought: so many kinds of liveliness under there, also hunkered down, also waiting.

———

Switching from skis to snowshoes, and getting exercise again after a long, stagnant indoor period, reminded me of something

I hadn't admitted to myself for fifteen years or so: I started running because I heard that it would get you high. I had come across this thrilling little rumor (in articles by journalists like myself), and wanted to see what that was like. The Sixties were over, I didn't particularly like the idea of drugs, but I certainly had nothing against having a good time. I began running, kept at it past the painful adaptation stage, began to enjoy it for itself, but also spent a lot of time carefully examining my responses: Is this it? Did I get off yet, am I finally high?

I never quite was. The high never happened—or if it did, was too subtle for sensibilities as coarse as mine. I had some very enjoyable times running the roads, but nothing particularly transcendent seemed to be happening. (The only thing I transcended was my expectations for myself—which really was a kick.) Running didn't get me high, but it got me interested, leading me on into swimming and competition and the rest of that whole athletic obsession. Or perhaps I did get high on training, on improving performance, but eventually the high wore off, and to increase the dose was beyond my physiological limits. Gradually I slowed down—literally, in recent years, from running to walking, as I now slow down from skiing to snowshoeing.

At the back of my mind, something was telling me that I was running right past the high: hurrying past the very transcendent moments I was seeking. If there were any such moments, they were coming at me too fast; I wasn't able to pay proper attention. Gross physical motion—expenditure of effort, rhythmic heavy work—does have a subtly intoxicating quality to it, and like any other junkie, I was trying to increase the intoxication by doing more, doing it faster, going at it harder. My urgent habits swirled me right past my goals.

I began doing stone work because I wanted to try getting high on that, too. Wanted to get stoned on work. The aim of a more sensory life, after all, is only to get stoned on simpler, subtler things. This might be called a homeopathic approach to pleasure. There are several other things I want to get stoned on, if I can learn to pay sufficient attention.

———

This morning I tracked myself to a standstill. Two days ago we got a gentle two-inch snow on top of hard crust, and yesterday when I walked the loop I put down a single set of fresh bootprints. Today as I walked along I was unthinkingly matching each of yesterday's footsteps with another, opposite-foot print: stepping beside yesterday's right-foot print with a left foot today, leaving matched pairs that looked like the places where someone had stopped and stood (or where someone had tried to bunny-hop around the loop). Then, startlingly, I came to a set where the other print was already in place: where I had in fact stopped yesterday, and stood still, probably to look at something. I never would have noticed the spot if I hadn't been unconsciously placing each step alongside the one from the day before.

It was the break in the pattern that made me realize I was tracking, if only myself. I'd never tried to track anything before. I'd taken passing notice of deer and turkey prints, and what I assumed were those of rabbits, mice, perhaps squirrels, but had never paid all that much attention to any of them. Everything else I dismissed as undecipherable dog tracks, probably from my own dogs. (There are eastern coyotes in these woods, and other dogs around, but I seldom see them in the flesh.) Among the dog tracks I can't separate out any distinct pattern anyway, just confusion where eight (or more?) canine-looking paws have torn up the snow. What wonderful mysteries. New snow lays down a clean sheet of paper, and the wildlife—the above-snow creatures, anyway—write on it. These stories can be read, but not yet by me.

Having the pattern jump out of my own track was a wonderful startlement, a flashing glimpse of how tracking might actually work. You must have to tune in to the pattern sufficiently to pick up its violation: the spike in the graph. The legendarily skilled tracking dogs obviously work from olfactory rather than visual patterns—although they're probably tuned in with every other sense, too, with everything they've got. If the spike in the pattern can jump out so vividly for preoccupied, inattentive me, what subtleties in it there must be for a professional dog.

I watch Molly as she thoroughly checks out a single twig extending into the path. (What other creature touched it, marked it, to rivet her attention so?) When she's through sniffing, she carefully straddles it and walks over it, deliberately dragging it along the length of her coat as she passes by. (What signal does this leave for the next creature?) I watch Pawnee work a wandering path off the trail. It's as if she is smelling her way along an invisible tunnel, one with almost palpable walls—like a blind man, but not with fingertips, with the nose alone. Not being privy to dog metaphors, I can't know how accurate this tunnel figure may be, but it's the one that occurs immediately as I watch. It makes me remember one consistent bit of marking behavior (the giving, rather than the getting, of scent) that has puzzled me in the past. Pawnee squats to pee in the trail; Molly immediately smells the spot, then pees on it herself: she's not trying to cancel Pawnee's scent, I think, but to blend with it, establishing a mixture, a structure of scents for intruding animals. (I mention this behavior to Chris. " 'We are us,' " she says, "that's what they must be saying.") I wonder if the dogs remember this loop in the woods not by picturing it but by somehow sniffing it in their memory, playing back a sequence of scents. We envision; do they ensmell? Surely they have some kind of mental map of the loop, but it must be a structure of smells. Dogs follow scent-lines: for them, scent must be much more connected with *place* than it is for us. (The aboriginal "songlines" of Australia—oral recitations that describe every geographical feature, and serve in lieu of maps—become an even richer idea for me now.)

Human beings are, I gather, much more sensitive to sound patterns than to scent patterns. Listening to the violinist hit the notes just right, I am driven to consider the powerful effect of hitting one wrong. Even I, knowing not the first note of music, carry sufficient patterning in my head that a sour note makes me wince. Perhaps the scent structures that dogs perceive are as firmly organized, and dogs are similarly startled by their disruption. From discarded clothing, a tracking dog can learn the scent of a stranger and then follow it—even through the soles of brand new shoes—across a "trackless" field. Smells must be as vivid for dogs as fluorescent paint is for us.

What keeps stirring my imagination about this tracking experience is that it wasn't the pattern but the break in it that I noticed. That's when I got that pleasurable little shock of a half-baked new thought: an idea being born, a tiny creative moment, carrying a kick like a chemical surge. Ideas are just chemicals anyway, Chris says. I like the image, chemicals surging around in the brain, waiting for a landing place to come along; something happens—a pattern is broken, perhaps—and receptor sites are uncovered: *pow*! a new thought. Maybe we are just the beasts with better brain chemistry. Different brain chemistry.

Eskimos are famous for having twenty-three terms for snow, or maybe it is sixty-eight. Some of those terms would surely fit the varieties of snow I have encountered this winter. I had never quite realized how variable the stuff was; I've learned more about it this winter than in fifteen years of reporting on winter sports for magazines, of skiing at a dozen different ski resorts every winter. I've learned it without ever thinking that that was what I was supposed to be thinking about, without giving it my conscious attention. It has moved me, perhaps, a quarter of an inch in the direction of being an expert, or Eskimo. (But how many more of these quarter-inch years do I have for such pursuits?)

Eskimos—aboriginal people in general—often seem like raving mystics to us. So does my veterinarian, not because he does or says mystical things but because of the way he moves his hands over my animals. He is obviously reading subtler signals from the animal than I am able to; he lives in a universe of subtler signals. I am sure this is the source of the expertise of the Eskimo, in mechanical matters or wildlife biology or anything else. Maybe this is what mysticism, or magic, always is. Perhaps mystics are just people who are extremely sensitive to these drugs of experience, who read the subtlest of signals (and, sometimes, are more or less overwhelmed by them). Who are able to pay attention to all these signals that go rushing past so fast. Friends have accused me of being a mystic for years, on no evidence. I've never had a mystical experience in my life. I think I'd like to. The mystics have always told us of transcendent moments. You can't force them, we are told. You have to be doing some other thing, engaging in some practice, and have them overtake you. If you're looking for them, they won't happen. They rush past, I think.

My mother died in the spring before I began building the wall. She contracted lung cancer late in her seventy-seventh year, and had six months of hard illness. My younger brother Dan nursed her at home in Texas for as long as he could. I flew down to see her, unprepared for the severity of her condition. When I drove her in for her radiation treatment, she was so debilitated and exhausted that on the way home I feared she might actually die in the car. I didn't know what a dying person would look like. Dan and I interrupted the radiation treatments to put her into the hospital, attempting to build her strength. She clearly needed professional care, and we began trying to decide the next step. The previous summer she had, with great foresight, picked out a nursing home near my other brother, Jud, and his wife, Marty, in Ohio. When the other possibilities were exhausted, she agreed that it was time to go there. I flew with her to Ohio and turned her over to Jud and Marty, who settled her into the new facility. She died there, peacefully, less than two months later.

She was a vigorous, even restless woman of high good humor and great independence, resolute and dependable. She could be unabashedly judgmental and at the same time a source of unequivocal love and support. In her later years arthritis slowed her considerably—souring, from time to time, her customary equanimity. By the time I reached Texas she was shockingly colorless and drawn, shrunken by a fifth in physical size from the summer before. After a night in the hospital, with intravenous nutrition and rehydration—and after she'd accepted the decision to move to a nursing home, which she knew full well would be her last change of residence—a transformation took place. Her skin tone acquired a ruddy glow, her eyes began to flash again, she looked twenty years younger. Old friends began parading through during visiting hours—not without emotion, since they knew she was leaving for good. She dealt with them easily, cheering them up and sending them on with a peculiar power and grace that I had never seen in her before. She told Dan and me a long string of funny stories about her family and growing up, some of them frankly bawdy. She was clearly free, now, to tell the truth, and was relishing it. The things she chose to tell were acute, salty, but unfailingly kind and generous, as if she didn't have time to waste on anger and blame.

Whatever was going on in that hospital room was so powerful that I couldn't take much of it at a time, would excuse myself and stagger out, exhausted. At the same time, I couldn't get enough of it, couldn't wait to go back in. It was as if waves of love were flowing out of her, burning clear enough, finally, that even I—numb, insulated, stone-walled as I was, and am— could feel it. I had never experienced anything like that, had not known anything like that existed. But I don't think it was mystical.

———

I awoke at three this morning from a strange dream of jealousy and hurt feelings, and couldn't immediately get back to sleep. I lay there thinking about a recent dream theory, which proposes that in sleep our brains are subject to random electrochemical activity, and dreams are simply the stories that our minds make up to explain the sensations we're feeling from that random activity. What if all emotions were just that, I thought, merely washes of random chemicals, not springing from any rational, objective, external thing in our lives. Not related *to* any rational, objective, external thing—except that in our determined, story-making way, we attach them to the details of our lives. What if our anger, for instance, isn't the result of some wound or imagined wound, some insufficiently processed event in our childhoods that was done or not done to us, but just from spurts of dopamine or serotonin or some other brain chemical, kicked loose by the physiology for its own unknowable reasons? What if we have no responsibility for any of it at all? And what if this making up of stories to explain things, this story-telling that we think we need to keep us sane, is actually the thing that makes us crazy? I enjoyed these thoughts so much that I lay awake for an hour more, waves of what must have been the chemicals of happiness washing through me, before I went back to sleep.

———

In real physics—as opposed to this business of simple mechanical laws that I keep calling by that name—the physicists have proposed the quark as the particle that is going to explain everything. The only problem is that the act of observing it changes it into something else. Or something like that: things go on in real physics that I don't pretend to understand. (And the physicists have gone several particles beyond the quark by now. That's okay: let the quark stand for whatever they're up to, particlewise.)

This sounds to me like another version of one of those wonderful old mythological quandaries like the Medusa's head, which Jason was able to lop off only by looking at its reflection in the polished mirror of his shield. The wonderful thing about the quark myth is that these guys have come up with the mathematics that prove it. To arrive at the concept of the quark by mathematics, and to believe that this is an objective, scientific, truthful explanation of what's at the heart of all matter, that it explains something about the universe, is as fabulous a demonstration of story-telling as anything that mankind— scientific or otherwise—has ever pulled off. It may say more, though, about the myth of the Medusa's head than about the nature of matter. Quarks sound to me like another story the scientists have made up to keep from going crazy—over the fact, for instance, that there's always going to be a smaller particle. By definition: to assume there's not, that there is in the end a smallest particle, is to box with God, isn't it? If there is not always going to be a smaller particle, whatever happened to infinity? Infinity being a mathematical concept we've come up with to ease some other wash of chemicals in the scientific brain.

———

"Let us gather facts," said the great French naturalist Buffon, "in order to have ideas." Stones are definitely facts. It had not occurred to me that I was carting them down the hill in order to stick them into an idea.

———

Here are some facts about the way the winter has actually gone. Christmas and the end of the year were unusually warm, for all my bitching, a little crusty snow here and there but generally light-jacket (as opposed to down-parka) weather. The new year started with a nice, dry, six-inch snowfall, followed by an Alberta Clipper and bright sun but howling winds, a windchill factor of thirty below. The pendulum swung back the next day, with a gentle two-inch snowfall, warming up to the freezing point by nightfall; the next day, forty degrees in bright sun to walk the loop. A high settled in, twenty degrees with bright sun, a couple of weeks of drought, the snow gradually turning to filthy ice. Then a *big* snow, a couple of feet, the kind of storm digging out from which is full of neighborly laughter and mutual support. Turns our little settlement into a true village.

And so on. It has indeed been a mild winter, holding off late into the fall and then blessing us with a succession of thaws. There was the one near the end of January, which we can almost pencil in on the calendar ahead of time—although no meteorologist has ever come up with an explanation of why it should happen so dependably at that time—and then a couple more in February, which is usually a sign that March will go on forever. March is always the big snow month anyway.

These are the details which I keep expecting finally to cohere somehow and let me see the winter more clearly. I spend part of every day now walking in these winter woods, flailing away at myself to pay more attention, to penetrate more deeply. There are such riches here, and I can't get at them. I make notes—the weather and whatever else I can fix my attention on—in an attempt to do so. I notice that the January thaw, for instance, has its usual weird effects on wildlife: I spot a huge porcupine thirty feet up in a tree, and smell skunk a few times. It doesn't seem right that mammals of that nature should be out this early.

When the thaw is on, I can feel heat blowing over the surface of the snow, and the woods begin to smell like woodsmoke. I can hear water trickling under the snow, a sign of life that's been withheld since mid-November. The wall begins to peek out of its cocoon; the snowcover softens so that even snowshoes sink, and I wade the loop in rubber boots, slurpily penetrating to mid-shin most of the way, acutely conscious of the tons of water that are up there on the hillside, poised to come rushing down if the thaw lasts too long.

"Good weather underneath the clouds," says the radio weatherman, of one of those gray, gloomy days when winter obviously will never end. To forestall my own gloom, I try selling myself the day. The harsh, bright colors of full sunlight are corny, I tell myself, calendar art; anybody can enjoy that. It takes a connoisseur to crack open one of these gray days and get pleasure out of it. In photography, I remind myself, over-exposure is murder: only in the muted grays, the fine tones, is delicacy of expression possible. (On the gray days of other seasons I pull off this self-swindle easily by pretending that it's Ireland out there, but grass has to be visible for this to work.) I stop at the top of the meadow and look down at the house: except for the green shutters, it's a black-and-white photograph. ("Everything looks worse," Paul Simon says, "in black and white.") And then a sleety little storm comes in, snowing so hard that if I tilt my head forward an inch, the snow down my neck feels like I'm standing in a cold shower.

Went out to exercise the dogs at four in the afternoon, heavily bundled against twenty-degree cold and harsh wind, but it wasn't as bad as predicted. I discovered the snow would bear my weight again, so I walked to the top of the hill pasture and ended up lying on the snow on my back, staring straight up into an uncanny blue twilight sky. After a while I sat up and began making an effort to observe precisely—the point on the horizon at which the sun had just disappeared, the estimated compass reading of the fall-line of the hill, and other such details—but soon lost patience with this naming of things. All I could see anyway was snow and woods and stone and sky and light.

Telling myself my story as I go along seems to help, maybe just as a way of assuring myself that I'm doing what I ought to be doing. But then I've been using words defensively all my life, to hold off experience. Words, I am beginning to think, are the specific barrier against seeing things clearly in these woods—and, at the same time, the only specific tool I have for penetrating the barrier. Perhaps this is the writer's curse. If I got to know these woods as an Eskimo would, maybe I'd no longer bother to write things down. Would know too much to write them down.

————

Incomprehensibly, a burst of rain last night, but the ultrahard crust holds, which makes the walking (with crampons) just fine. The rain has washed down the woods, bringing up the reds and browns, a shock in the middle of winter's monochrome. Those reds and browns are not lying, I assure myself; but where do they go between rains? The bumper sticker says, "Think globally, act locally"; for New England in mid-winter, that ought to be "think geologically, act meteorologically." Or maybe it is that you have to think globally after all, think about the planet's attitude in space, the irrevocability of its motion, to get you through to spring. Think solar-systemically. Not geopolitically, anyway. Geometeorologically?

Closing my eyes to sleep, I try to keep all words out of my head—concentrating hard, pulling up and starting over again whenever a word comes floating into my consciousness. I can manage it for only a few seconds at a time, and then the words come pouring back in. If I succeed for longer, what I get instead of words is a picture, usually of a particular place from memory. My mind immediately starts making up a story about the place, and then I'm dreaming, and I'm asleep. It is as if the consciousness insists on being given a story to entertain it before I can let go of it and sleep. I need to see that it is safely occupied. (My soul to keep?) I'm amazed at how hard it is to keep the words out, how tight I have to screw my mental muscles, hold a tension in my mind. Shouldn't it be that I just relax and let the words go?

————

Here's a place in the snow where some animal has dug down to bare earth, moss and other fragments scattered around, the snow dug up, scooped out, hollowed. I don't know why. The dogs spot it much sooner than I, naturally, and are more intrigued, more interested. There's a scenario here, a drama going on at this place, but I can't make it out. I make a note to pick up some books on tracking. A little farther on I come across another disturbance on the snow, a rumpled spot, at each side of which is the clear print where wingtips have brushed the surface. Some good-sized bird has flapped its wings here, either in landing or taking off, or just in swooping low to strike. For some reason the notion lodges in my head that it was a grouse (which doesn't strike), but I don't know what association puts it there.

My approach in matters such as this has always been to see the marks, go get a book that will tell me what happened, then go back and look at the marks again. (And then run tell somebody all this stuff I now know.) I haven't done that yet with these woods, have been reluctant to research their biology, their botany. I've done that with too many subjects, and am sick of it. I want to get this place through my pores somehow. It isn't working yet; I am still the tunnel-visioned Westerner, focusing on details. Still not an Eskimo. I don't know what to look for. I swear that in this new year I will slow down, find out. Mindfulness, that's the ticket. Any day now.

———

Mid-February: new harnesses for my snowshoes, and a gloriously warm thirty-degree late afternoon, still an acceptable level of light at three-thirty. In fact, I realize spring light is on the way, it's coming down at new angles, the sun in a slightly different place. The long stretch down the hill at the end of the loop is now backlit with a surprising glow. The surface of the snow is covered with chaff of some kind, little yellow fleur-de-lis shapes: vegetal stirrings, indicating that in deepest winter some kind of botanical process is still—or already—going on. Also hemlock needles and tiny cones, and piles of sawdust, at the foot of dead trees, from woodpeckers. The later into the spring it gets, the more of this detritus is sprinkled over the top of the snow. After a while it gets so trashy that I welcome each new snowfall. Neatens up the place.

We've had a two-week period when the temperature bounced up above the freezing point most days, weakening the snow crust so that it will just hold up the dogs, making them walk very carefully, paws spread out wide. The weakened crust really cools them out: if they try to run, give in to their natural exuberance, they go crashing through and must flounder along, crotch-deep front and rear. They can't even wag their tails without their hindquarters suddenly dropping through the crust. After twenty minutes or so of walking across this precarious surface, their tails and ears and heads are drooping, their body language depressed; they've been deliberately holding down their enthusiasm for so long that they begin to look like they've been beaten. They're exhausted.

———

Bird song at dawn, as another thaw kicks in and holds. (There's probably a lot of bird life around on winter dawns, but I don't stand around outside listening to it.) By noon it has turned into an absolutely crystalline, deep-blue, clear-sky, windless February day, unimaginably clear and bright. The clarity comes, I believe, from the deepness of the blue above, its darkness. An art director friend says she makes the mistake of always seeing the snow as too blue, or too pink. Poor art directors, yanked out of nature by their craft.

This morning the woods are wet again, and I can definitely

see the pink haze. The woods are still basically gray, but you can pick up the tinge, the hue, of growth. (Actually, willows show it first, and the color is pale yellow instead of pink: just the first hint of light against the gray.) When I come outdoors I see nothing but gray at first, but the longer I look, the more color comes welling up. It's as if my black-and-white eyes are being awakened from their winter sleep, as more color begins to appear in stuff that for the past three months I have dismissed as dead gray. This is wrong, of course, there's always plenty of color, even in the snow; see my art director friend. Maybe in deep winter I have, more or less despairingly, tuned it out. Maybe true color is just another one of those other rich experiences out there that I never quite have.

The pink haze seems early this year. Is it because it has been a mild winter and an early spring, or is it that pushing at myself to see more for the past year has made me a little better at picking up the color? Maybe it's working. Maybe my eyes aren't as grayed-out this winter as they were last winter. Maybe the riches don't come from what you're paying attention to. From what you think you're paying attention to.

I've never learned how to focus my attention, just as I never learned to study in school, only to read the books—the stories—that pulled my attention out of me. Actively focusing attention, coming up with enough mental energy to keep attention focused on something, was entirely too much effort. I didn't know how to do it. I still don't. I want to be able to step back and let the sheer beauty of this place overwhelm me, carry me passively along, but clearly that's all wrong, a sure way to tune out: what I have to do to see into the woods is dig into the details (as Mies van der Rohe pointed out long ago— quoting, I'm sure, someone else). To focus on detail I take notes, attempting to write down the riches of the woods, trying to convince myself that I have gotten those riches. But I haven't, I never have. I don't know enough, don't see enough, don't know how to see. Don't know what I've seen, what was going on, until I get back and start writing about it, telling myself the story: debriefing myself on the experience. Every time that I see a little bit more, it tells me there are worlds and worlds more to see, deeper yet. The pleasure I get when I see a little tells me that all pleasure, all happiness, lies in seeing more. Whenever I manage to see some tiny bit, I always say to myself again, yes, that's the way I wish I lived: seeing these things.

What I come up into these woods for, I hope, is their calm advice. The way nature works is the way it is going to work, willy nilly, which seems to me as clear a piece of wisdom as I'm likely to get. Nature obeys the laws of the physical universe. I would like to. I fail, much of the time, almost exactly to the degree I insert my conscious intent into the process. It is my contribution to the human condition. Our silly failure to respect those laws is exactly what defines us as a race, I think: that human urge we have to push things a step too far. The urge that makes us either hard to love or entirely lovable, I'm never sure which.

Last of February: twenty degrees, hard crust, crampons. Stink of skunk. A bright, increasingly powerful sun. Last night the weatherman said that red-winged blackbirds have been seen in Boston, sap is running in southern New Hampshire. Hans says he's heard the chickadee's spring call. I've pretty well verified that the vegetal stirrings are the coverings of maple buds—at least there seem to be more of them under maples than under birches, where I originally thought they were coming from. Sap buckets are appearing on roadside trees. If you walk right up and look at twigs, you can see that the buds are coming. But that requires deciding to see if spring is yet on the way, and I hate to get so damned programmatic about things. I like it best the other way, when the pink haze overtakes me, getting my attention.

[15]

EQUINOX:

GOOD AIR

As months go, March is mostly a delaying tactic. By then we've gotten all the good out of a winter that we're going to get; coziness itself has begun to cloy, and let's not even talk about icy invigoration. Garrison Keillor says that God invented March in order that people who don't drink can find out what a hangover is like. It didn't take us many New England winters to figure out that March is the time to get the hell out of here.

So we bail out and head for the Caribbean, flinging garments (of repentance and otherwise) as we go. After some years of experimentation we have settled on one scruffy little island, offering almost nothing but itself. You wouldn't like it, we say to curious acquaintances. Hans sometimes comes along, this year accompanied by Lynne, the local newspaper reporter who has agreed to marry him. Hans is a Dutch skin-diver who is passionate about adding to his life-list of birds. Before he came with us the first time, he asked a travel agent about our choice of islands. Well, the agent said with a grimace, unless you speak Dutch and like to dive, or are one of those bird-watchers, there's not a damned thing to do there. She got it exactly right.

Getting there is an all-day ordeal, involving the usual three or four flights on progressively smaller and more tattered aircraft, with progressively more conspicuous oil leaks. The day is spent mostly in tedious negotiations with multilingual but curiously uninformative airline personnel and customs officials, and long waits in stultifying, fly-blown terminals, wearing inappropriate clothing. I traveled for years for professional reasons, and have come to hate every moment of it. Getting to our island is not my favorite way to spend a day.

But we step off the last flight into the softest air ever breathed, and get to the hotel in time for a congratulatory rum punch—barefooted—on the terrace before bedtime. The tropical night sky is such a glorious shock, after New England in March, that we keep asking each other for reality checks. And the next morning, in brilliant early sunlight, I will stroll down to the beach in very little clothing and slip into the sea. There I will swim down only a fathom or two before I am surrounded by friendly fish, and I will know that for a little while it won't be March anymore.

———

I have only one real talent, which is to swim upside down. I love to hang that way in salt water, my head (masked and snorkel-tubed) toward the bottom, my feet (finned) pointed toward the surface. The view is better. I swim around upside down and backward, as comfortable deep beneath the surface as on it, at least for as long as my breath holds out. This is a talent of which I am immodestly proud, although I can take no credit for it. It is a pure gift, an accident, not developed through any arduous learning curve. It is the best thing I do. Others have a talent for playing musical instruments, for hitting golf balls, for picking out the spikes in patterns. For putting others, or themselves, at ease. I have a talent for hanging upside down in the water. It is of no use except for my personal pleasure. I would rather do it than anything else I know to do with my body, except the one other thing.

What it allows me to do is cruise around underwater looking at fish. With scuba tanks I wouldn't have to keep coming up for air, but I don't like all the paraphernalia, and refuse to do that anymore. My way is more vigorous and, I think, more fun. I'm also a strong swimmer, which allows me to dive deep and stay down long, increasing my enjoyment. So I basically spend my winter vacation upside down in a warm saline solution, a hundred yards or so offshore, over or alongside a reef, watching fish. Chris enjoys snorkeling almost as much as I do, and it has become what we go to the Caribbean for.

In between these vacations, I always forget how powerful this pleasure is for me. When I go back and slip beneath the surface for the first time, and, in my mind, greet the fish, I am always surprised to rediscover what a water person I am: how directly and specifically the water is my element, what a familiar and reassuring embrace it has for me. I've loved it all my life. My mother loved it as much as I do. Jud taught me to swim, but Gwen was the one who taught me to love the water so.

———

Hans and Lynne meet us for breakfast on an open-air flagstone terrace with a woven palm roof. Bananaquits flit about the palm fronds, stealing jam from breakfast tables. Sandpipers of some kind skitter back and forth along the line of surf, turning over small stones. (They're called turnstones, Hans tells us.) Small fishing boats head out to sea. Crabs scuttle among the rocks of the nearby jetty, frigate birds soar overhead, terns and brown pelicans work their way along the shore plunging occasionally after fish. The Dutch serve magnificent coffee.

We decide on a recovery day, easing into our holiday week at the hotel beach. Amply sunscreened and well supplied with reading material, we swim and snooze and swim again, glorying in the warmth and light. Chris finds a school of horse-eye jacks circling a coral head in which a spotted moray eel has intertwined itself. Eels are supposed to be nocturnal, and the jacks seem almost to be shading it. (They will remain in the same spot all afternoon, and will be there again the next day, although the eel will be gone. What are they after?) I amuse myself by swimming down to where small, delicately shaded florettes of pink and brown poke up through the bottom sand or from holes in the coral. They are, I think, the feeding tentacles of some kind of sea worm; if I startle them with the current from a wave of my hand, they simply disappear, sucked back into the hole so quickly they seem to snap into invisibility.

I cruise parallel to the shore for a while, hovering over the reef, looking for interesting things to dive down to: hanging at the surface to catch my breath, then dropping down a level to where the next species is at play, or work. Then I get out and lie on the beach, and watch the frigate birds and pelicans hover above us, doing the same thing. "Fishes are virtually underwater birds," says our guidebook. It's a nice thing to think about while lying on a beach: both creatures so liberated, dimensionally, in their respective mediums. When I'm swimming in thirty feet of crystal-clear Caribbean water, it is like nothing so much as flying in a giant blue room. Swimming over the edge of the drop-off, where the bottom falls precipitously away, is a little like pushing off from a cliff face in a hang glider. (The real reason I don't scuba dive anymore is that when I swim upside down, or cut any other didoes, the heavy tank throws me off balance. There's too much drag from all that gear; I'm sleeker when I just go swim. Chances to feel sleek aren't that easy to come by.)

I settle into the shade with a second rum punch, an open notepad on my lap, thinking I will observe and record these thundering profundities. (Alcohol often does this to me.) Here I am aswirl in wildlife, but nothing makes its way down onto the page. The rum punches do not kick in, the impulse to make notes dies a merciful death. It is the vacation that kicks in instead, the beep-beep of brain wave activity slowing to a gentle, grinning hum.

Later, we sit on the balcony to watch the sunset, which comes on, as it will in the tropics, with a clash of cymbals, fully orchestrated. Backlit purple clouds shade toward an uncanny chocolate brown, toward colors unnamed and unnameable, medleys of refracted light we've never seen before. Venus and Jupiter emerge, shockingly, in the vast, vast late afternoon sky. I struggle with the globe in my head, trying to envision where on it this place actually is, and where home is in relation to it, while the melon ball of the sun—in this fruity, moist soft paradise—slips beneath a prussian-blue sea. The tropics are a sweet shop. Plenty of molecules around. There certainly is good air in this place.

One year Willy and Liz came here with us. The four of us went for a swim off a west-facing beach in late afternoon. The reef was well offshore, in water twenty feet deep or more, and Chris and I were swimming perhaps thirty yards farther out than Willy and Liz. The slanting sun cast long rays underneath the water, reducing visibility. I spotted a backlit shape out of the corner of my eye that looked vaguely sinister and, not wanting

to give myself or anyone else a fright, suggested casually to
Chris that we head back toward Willy and Liz. As we turned
to do so, a school of dolphins was suddenly swimming below,
beside, and among the four of us. There must have been twenty-
five of them, rolling and tumbling along at a good clip, headed
south. I put my head down and sprinted after them, not to
chase them but because I wanted to stay in their company a
moment or two longer. Then they were gone. We joined up
with Willy and Liz, all four of us jabbering with exhilaration
and gratitude, and swam slowly in to shore. Swimming with
dolphins, now, that's a high.

I came out of the water babbling about how quickly my
reaction had changed from fear to joy. The unidentified shape
moments before had made me distinctly anxious. When I saw
the dolphins, though, that anxiety was instantly replaced with
the happy certitude that the dolphins were not only benign but
positively friendly. My first glimpse of the dolphin silhouette
had said to me, for reasons I didn't understand, "welcome."

One of Willy's areas of expertise is oceanography, and he
had an interesting story that helped explain my reaction. He
had been on scientific dives when sharks were a scary presence.
A scientist had given him a rule of thumb. The major source
of the shark's propulsion is its vertical tail fin; when it swims,
the motion of the tail causes the head to swing back and forth,
from side to side. In dolphins and other aquatic mammals, the
driving tail is horizontal, so their swimming motion causes the
head to nod up and down. You can tell them apart instantly,
from a distance: the shark is saying "no, no," as it swims along;
the dolphin is saying "yes."

With Hans and Lynne we rent a car and, wincing at the ex-
pense, set out to do the whole island in one day. We drive

around the windward side, watching the surf crash. (Swimming is dangerous here; "no sturdiness PLEASE" says the brochure.) We visit seaside caves with prehistoric ideograms, the slave pens by the salt flats, the stone ruin of an abandoned lighthouse at the north end of the island. We spend a quiet half-hour at each of two watering holes in the bird sanctuary; while we're at the second, some kind of sea eagle comes swooping in, lands twenty yards away from where we sit, and strides purposefully around in the cactus scrub, fierce-eyed and cocky. Hans is stunned by his luck.

We stop at a secluded cove for a swim and a picnic lunch. A cool front had come through in the night, wiping away the usual puffy fair-weather clouds. I don mask and fins and go underwater to check the entry point for spiny sea urchins, dangerous to bare feet. There are none. I swim out through swarms of parrotfish, angelfish, trunkfish straight out of an animated cartoon. I surface fifty yards out to clear my mask, and look around me. I am midway between two black volcanic cliffs, treading brilliant Caribbean blue water under a perfectly clear blue sky, and a flight of flamingoes chooses that moment to swirl across the mouth of the cove, flying in that curious undulating single file they seem to prefer. It is my turn to be stunned by my luck.

We picnic in the shade of a thorn tree, iguanas scuttling about our feet, begging scraps. A mother goat and her quintessentially adorable kid also join us, somewhat nervously. Then we see why, as a big black billy comes over to dissuade them from fraternizing with the enemy. There are feral goats all over the island, wandering the roads, ducking off into the cactus as you drive by. They're cute and charming and a mild nuisance (and, I suspect, a principal ingredient of any dish labeled barbecue). This male is not cute. He is utterly dramatic, coal black with perfectly mad blue-white eyes, a jittery electricity about him, the wildest, most demonic animal I have ever laid eyes on. He bounds around us in a weirdly ritualistic way; one can almost hear the druidic pipes to which he dances. In him there are several thousand years of mythology on display. I never dreamed those dusty stories could have sprung from such a preternaturally real and vivid creature.

Avian cocktail fact: migrating birds tend to have dark wing tips. Hans told me about this. Pigmentation is a kind of strengthener. Feathers that appear white are weakest (and, I assume, lightest in weight). When a bird flies long distances, its tip feathers are the ones most battered, that get the most wear. Evolution has gradually dyed the tip feathers—"almost like dipping them in paint," Hans says, to make them last longer. I love stories like that.

Birds seen on the island by Hans (Lynne handed me his list): bananaquit, grassquit, brown pelican, flamingo, sea eagle, greater yellowlegs, common egret, tropical mockingbird, turkey vulture, pearly-eyed warbler, turnstone plover, yellow warbler, great blue heron, black-necked stilt, boat-tailed grackle, Wilson's warbler, yellow-shouldered parrot, bittern or green heron, crow, least sandpiper, drumlin (peep), red-tailed hawk, and nonspecified terns, ground doves, pigeons, and orioles. Many of these were seen at the sanctuaries, but it is not necessary to go that far for all of them. For a good part of one morning Chris and I watched a great blue heron as it hid in the shadows among the pilings under the hotel restaurant. It would stand stock still while the surf washed in at its feet, spot some prey, take a step out into the sun and spear it, step back into hiding to gulp it down.

The bananaquits are back in force, after dropping off in numbers for a couple of years. A cook tells us that the new chef is responsible. The old chef was not charmed by the little birds, and hid all the sugar and jam; the new chef likes them, and restored their sweets. Guests feed bread scraps to the turnstones, making them bold enough to flit over a low stone wall into the restaurant in search of hand-outs. Tourists also feed the local fish, making them increasingly aggressive. If you hold out your hand to them underwater, they will come to you; if you don't have food, they may nip your fingers. They too are being pulled into the tourist industry, their natural patterns disrupted. We are colonizing them, third-worlding them. I don't want to be precious about this. I like watching the fish come in to get fed, even enjoy, with a shiver, the nasty snick-snick feeding sounds they make in their frenzy. But it does work at the back of one's head: here we go again, not being wise.

―――――――

We buy guidebooks to help us recognize species of fish. (Some scuba divers carry waterproof plastic cards for reference underwater. Holding your breath, however, doesn't give time for reading material.) When we come out of the water, we dig out the books and look up what we've just seen, mostly in order to talk to each other about these things. We probably see two or three times as many species underwater as we do above.

I'm continually disappointed in myself that I don't know the names of things, that I'm not able to identify all the trees and plants and birds back home, for example. In the islands this naming of things becomes a little obsessive. I find it a distracting way to pay attention. The turnstones are nondescript little speckled birds until they fly; then they suddenly blossom with a nice paint job, with brown and white stripes in a striking pattern. The name doesn't tell you anything about that. I watch them scuttle back and forth in the edge of the surf on toothpick legs, considering that each tiny toe has its own system of tendons, muscle fibers, calcium gates, actomyosin cross-bridges. Smaller particles there, too. The best part of being here may not be the fish or even the water itself, but the patterns on the water. Or the color of it. Trying to do the whole island in one day is a mistake, I think, seeking gross experience rather than fine. Swimming with the dolphins was truly breath-taking, but the feel of the air on my skin is also terrific, and sufficient. I would now like to abandon the *Guinness Book of World Records* approach to vacationing.

To see is to forget the name of the thing one sees, Paul Valéry said. After a voluptuous afternoon nap I sit groggily on our hotel room balcony, watching a tern at work. It travels methodically along the shoreline from north to south, circling and circling as it goes, then plunges suddenly into the sea after its prey—although I must have watched it for ten minutes before I began to see even that much pattern. Its preferred hunting altitude is about thirty feet; when it spots something and decides to dive, it jerks abruptly upward to gain another ten feet or so before folding its wings and plummeting. Is this extra fillip to gain more momentum for the dive? To get a better sight line on its prey? Perhaps as an evasive maneuver, putting its shadow in a new place, deceiving the fish about its intention? I never do figure that part out, but the pattern etches itself on my eye: swirling circles repeated tirelessly, the sudden swerve upward, the folded wings and the dive and splash. It is the best moment I have with birds the entire trip. I don't know it is a tern at the time, have to ask Hans later what kind of bird it was. The name that can be named is not the name, says the *Tao*.

For a long time I sit and watch the tern with my mind God knows where, unable to think about it, unable to see what I am looking at. Unable to notice; just watching this circling, circling bird, charmed by it, lulled, hypnotized, loving its flight but unable to tell why, watching it circle and swoop and dive. The moment the pattern registers is the moment I see that the upward fillip is repeated, is also part of the scheme: the quirk in it, the spike in the circle. The interruption that raises the question, and therefore raises my interest: the receptor site for the chemicals circulating in my brain, the idea looking for a place to land.

––––––––

The ferocious intensity of that pitch-black goat keeps coming back, a wedge into my imagination: a first glimpse, for me, of how mythology might happen. Maybe it was seeing him under a thorn tree, poking up out of dead volcanic stone, at seaside. Maybe it was the sea itself whispering in the background, that corny old folk stuff about how it, too, is an entity, the sea as mother. I never felt that before, never allowed those metaphors to flesh themselves out in my imagination. Earth as entity, mountain as god, nature as presence; none of those huge overarching pantheistic categories, I never twigged to any of that.

The sea as entity, that living palpable thing out there that heaves and sighs and carries in its bosom all that quivering protein, all those little live things. That has its own sweet smell, and air, and plays so wonderfully with the light. Funny how it has taken me fifty years to get one of mankind's oldest, simplest ideas. In school I had of course encountered the idea of the sea as goddess (in "primitive" times), a whimsical little idea in library books, but never any sense that human minds would actually comprehend the body of the sea itself that way.

The funny thing is, I never liked the sea. I liked to swim, liked to be in it, but as landscape it always bored me stiff. Nothing but a damned flat line on the horizon; I preferred mountains, wanted some *relief*. I guess I was looking too far off into the distance again, should have been looking down at the wavelets lapping at my feet. If I'd gone at the sea in the Western way, researching it, reading books, zeroing in on specifics, I never would have gotten it. I never have gotten things that way.

I got it—or I will get it, if I ever do—through my pores, my skin, the way the fish get me. You can't "touch" a fish: reach and it is gone. If you make physical contact, it is by the fish's choice. Or when you reach for a fish, you touch it long before your fingers are anywhere close: the fish picks up the movement, the feel of your approach, from currents in the water, and reacts. Looked at as physics, this transmission of "touch" through the fluid medium is perfectly clear and understandable—an experiment you can play with (delightfully) in the lab of the Caribbean.

But to truly get it, to accommodate this operative principle of the sea and make one's mind work that way, involves feeling it: feeling it come back the other way, in the pressure from the fish. To feel a fish swim by is to know finally that there is a web between us, that we are in fact in contact with all those creatures from the moment we get into the sea. What I have to do now is learn how to come back up—into the less dense medium where I am forced, most of the time, to live—with that web intact.

If I ever succeed, I dream, then I will be connected: numbness gone, insulation removed, eligible, finally, for a more sensory life. Or I will finally manage to crowbar my own ego out of the center of the universe and for the first time be able to pay attention to something other than my own sweet, seductive self.

———

Flying home, vacation over, I suffer a particularly virulent spell of travel-hatred in the men's room of the airport in San Juan. The place is clean enough, but has an overlay of tropical stickiness: sweat on the tiles, a layer of soap scum on the metal fixtures under gray, slightly inadequate fluorescent lights. A couple of drunks belch and sway as they slick back pomaded hair in the scuzzy mirrors. We've been en route for six hours, and damp socks are sagging around my ankles. The concept of "freshening up" is only a wistful dream. We have two more hours to wait, then another long flight, followed by an hour's drive home. Once we get on the next flight, we will fetch out of the beach bag the even hotter and sweatier New England clothing that we'll need the moment we land.

For some reason I think of Gwen's last flight. She was a medium-sized, even ample woman, turned by the cancer into a tiny crone. We used a wheelchair to get her to the plane in San Antonio, and an ambulance would be waiting in Dayton. She sank into the seat beside me and immediately fell asleep, exhausted by the thirty-minute trip to the airport. I pretended to read, worrying again that she might have some terrible sinking spell in flight, where I could do nothing for her.

There was a stopover in St. Louis to service the plane, and everyone else disembarked. Our seats were directly opposite the galley, and suddenly a large door on that side of the airplane was thrown open, letting in a cold blast of wind and blowing rain. I started to get outraged, then realized that I had a bright little pair of eyes at my elbow; my mother, looking somehow like a tiny squirrel, was following every move the crew made.

They yanked out the used food containers and slammed new ones into place with a terrific crashing and banging of doors and trays; she sat there grinning, absolutely riveted by the process. As soon as they finished and shut the exterior door, she sank back into sleep. She always loved to travel.

I rejoin Chris in the airport in Puerto Rico, bitching about fatigue. I mention my queasy spell in the men's room, and that for some reason I had found myself thinking of Gwen. I could be a good traveler too, I say, if I could just be as interested in the men's room as Gwen had been in the servicing of that plane. Well, Chris says, maybe if you knew it was the last time you'd ever see a Puerto Rican men's room. . . .

———

Home again, back in the woods on snowshoes, slopping along on wet, slushy snow—a fairly dramatic change of texture. Forty-five degrees at noon, dogs gleefully home from the kennel, a beautiful day, all's right with the world. It's been ten days since I was up here last, and the snow has melted so fast that I can barely see the packed-out trail where I have looped this loop all winter long. I had expected that the snowshoes would pack out a harder trail, something set up in ice so it wouldn't thaw as quickly as the rest of the snow. But everything seems to be melting at about the same rate. I don't seem to be having as much effect on these woods as I had expected.

I doubt I'll start another wall. Contrary to my epic plans, I will not be stringing lines of stone hither and yon across the yard and around the fields, constructing terraces and courtyards. Stone work needs a certain obsessiveness, and I seem to have come out the other end of it without achieving that. I would love to have had it happen, to have become an obsessive wall-builder, laying up ever more intricate and beautiful constructs of stone—becoming a true master—but I didn't, and probably won't. It is perfectly lovely and satisfying work to do, but there's no shortage of that around here, and some of it nags at me even harder than the wall does. I have always enjoyed my obsessions, all of them, and realize now that in stone work I missed a great one. It didn't seize me hard enough. It seems to have let me go.

It gave me another one, though, to take its place: it nailed me out of doors. It held me there long enough for that to take permanent hold, the need to be out there in the light where the molecules are moving around. It made the outside of this place sufficiently more important than the comfortable and distracting inside. That, I think, is an obsession worth holding on to. Another pearl of great price.

I stop to make a note about that. Then, as my breath begins to quiet in the silent woods, I pick up a squeaking, creaking sound, growing steadily louder, that makes the hair stand up on the back of my neck. I snap my head up and overhead, oh my God, here come three hundred, five hundred, a thousand Canada geese, maybe fifteen hundred, stretching across the sky in a succession of vees. Largest flight I've ever seen. Underlit from reflection off the snow, a skyful of silver arrowheads, bound due north for the summer to come. A skyful of physiology, riding the physics of the air toward the pole. Riches, riches, everywhere, just for the paying of attention. Even in two stones on one, one stone on two.